ZEN

FOR BEGINNERS™

Judith Blackstone

and

Zoran Josipovic

Illustrated by

Naomi Rosenblatt

Orient BlackSwan

ORIENT BLACKSWAN PRIVATE LIMITED

Registered Office
3-6-752, Himyatnagar
Hyderabad 500 029 (A.P), India
Email: centraloffice@orientblackswan.com

Other Offices
Bangalore / Bhopal / Bhubaneshwar / Chennai / Ernakulam / Guwahati
Hyderabad / Jaipur / Kolkata / Lucknow / Mumbai / New Delhi / Patna

Cover Design : Suzetta Bozzi
Cover Art : Naomi Rosenblatt

Published by arrangement with
Writers and Readers Limited
P O Box 29522
London N1 8 FB

First Published by Orient Longman Private Limited 2001
Reprint 2003
First Orient Blackswan Impression 2008

ISBN 13: 978-81-250-2048-6
ISBN 10: 81-250-2048-9

Printed In India at
Multifold
Chennai 600 085

Published by
Orient Blackswan Private Limited
160, Annasalai, Chennai 600 002
Email: chennai@orientblackswan.com

TABLE OF CONTENTS

FOR OUR SISTERS,
BILJANA, TIJANA, LEAH,
AND BROTHER, DANIEL.

Cast of Characters

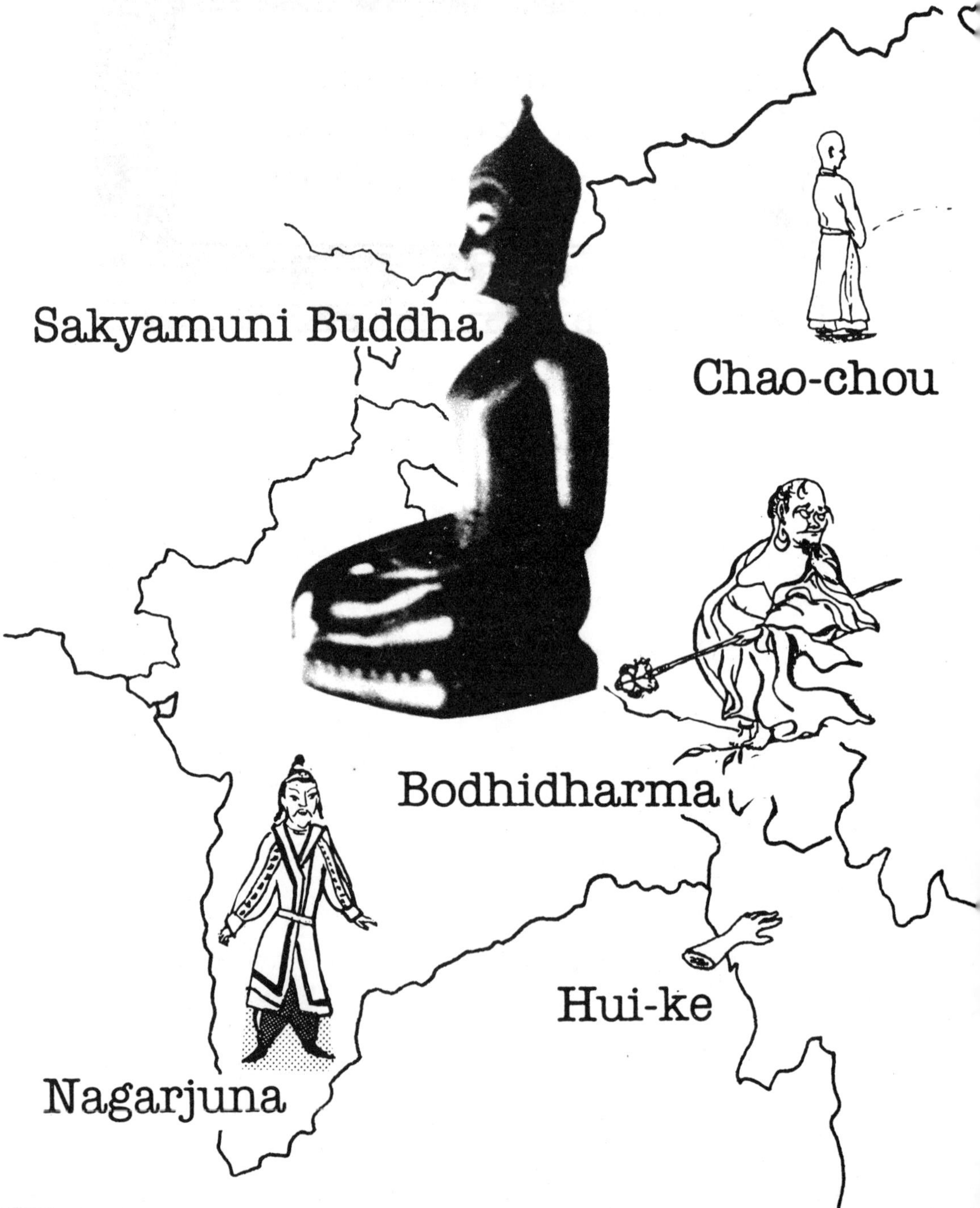

Po-chang Huai-hai
Dogen
Nan-ch'uan
Ma-tsu
Shih-tou
Eisai
Tung-shan
Hakuin
PACIFIC OCEAN
Hui-neng
Rinzai

why did Bodhidharma come from the west?
The cypress tree in the garden.

INTRODUCTION

When we were asked, by the illustrator, to write this book, we right away said, "No".

First of all, any book on Zen starts out at a disadvantage. Zen cannot be described in words, it is an experience more basic than the level of conceptual thinking. It has to do with our innermost life, what the Zen masters call

"OUR ORIGINAL FACE, BEFORE OUR PARENTS WERE BORN"

which is gone as soon as we analyse it. Zen is not something we can learn, or even become, because we are already it, we can only be it.

Second, this is supposed to be a light book, but Zen is a heavy subject—personally, we think it may be the heaviest subject on the planet—it's about ultimate reality, liberation from pain and confusion, our greatest potential.

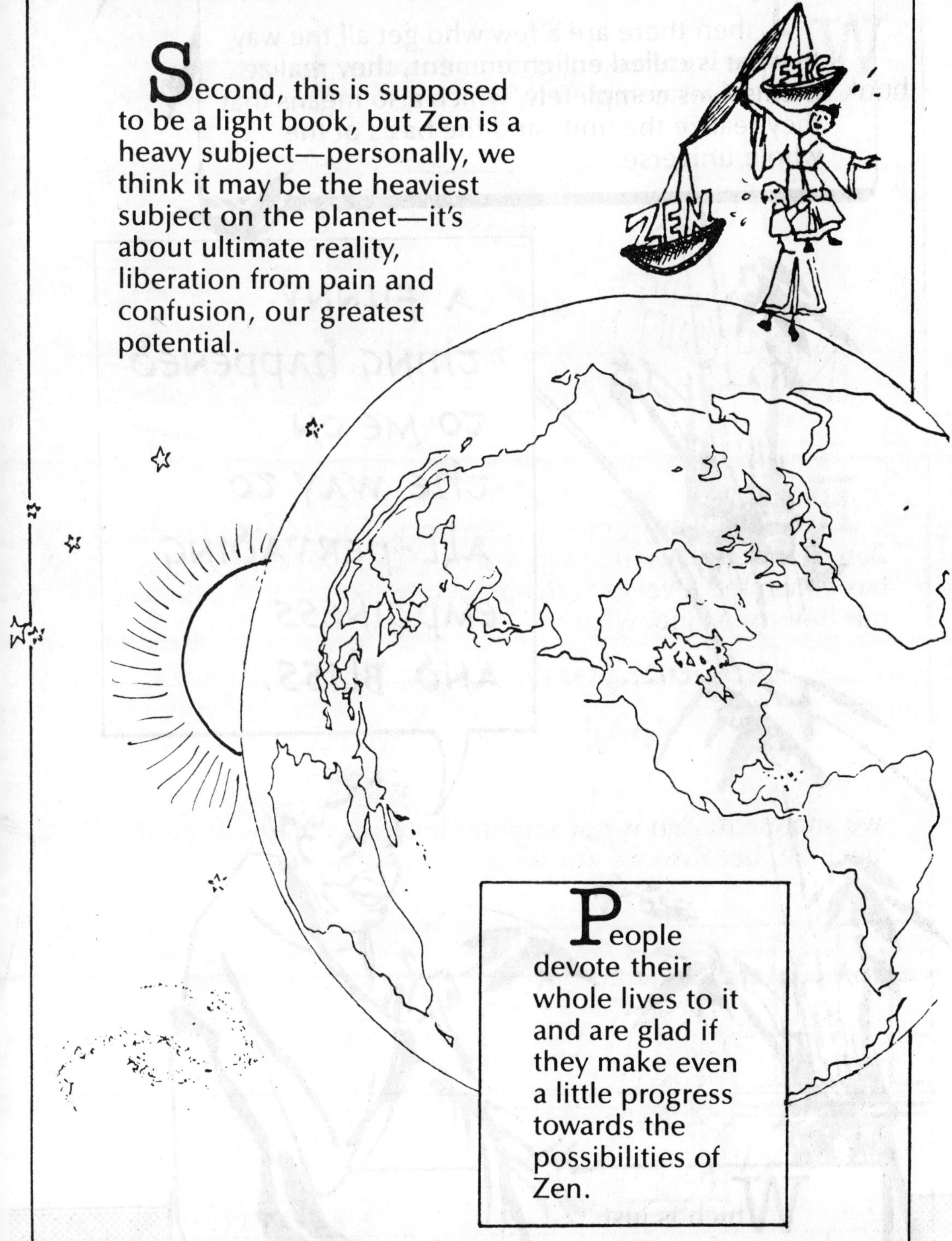

People devote their whole lives to it and are glad if they make even a little progress towards the possibilities of Zen.

Then there are a few who get all the way to what is called enlightenment, they realize themselves completely, which also means that they realize the unity and the basis of the whole universe.
A FUNNY THING HAPPENED TO ME ON THE WAY TO ALL-PERVADING EMPTINESS AND BLISS.
Which is just by way of saying that if there is something funny about this book, it's not the fault of the subject matter.

And third, these enlightened masters are the only ones who should open their mouths at all about Zen. Anyone else is liable to make more confusion about it than less. We knew if we wrote this book, we could put in it only the most introductory information, that can be found in other books that were written by people with more experience than ourselves (and that's what we did).

so the real title of this book is

Which brings us to the reason we finally decided to write it, the title. It's a very appropriate title, because Zen masters speak a lot about "beginner's mind". In Zen practice, we are trying to become beginners, to experience life without the interference of our whole accumulation of opinions and ideas.

This doesn't mean that we should be stupid, or in some kind of trance, far from it. The Buddhists count cognition as one of our six senses, and they definitely mean for us to know what's happening, but directly, the way things are reflected in a clear mirror.

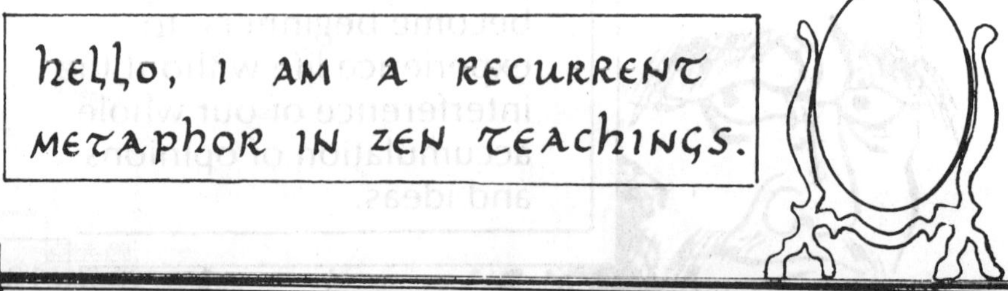

For example, if we look at a tree, and we have beginner's mind, we won't have to get into a whole dialogue with ourselves about how it's an oak tree, there's a lot of them around here, once I fell out of a tree just like this one, maybe if I sell the oak dresser in my room I can go to Bermuda, and so on—we just see the tree.

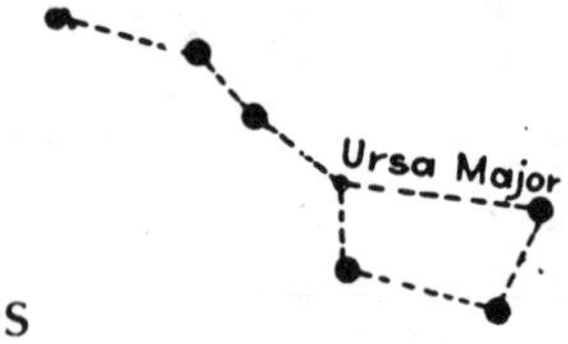

And then, because all of our senses are free to focus together, without distraction, we become aware of all kinds of things we otherwise wouldn't notice–we can even sense that the life in the tree is not so different from our own, and at that point, we are reaching a level of perception which the Zen masters call "intimacy", or "no separation". Zen teaches that when we are most aware, there is no feeling of separation between subject and object. Like the space inside and outside of a vase, we experience the space inside and outside of ourselves as continuous.

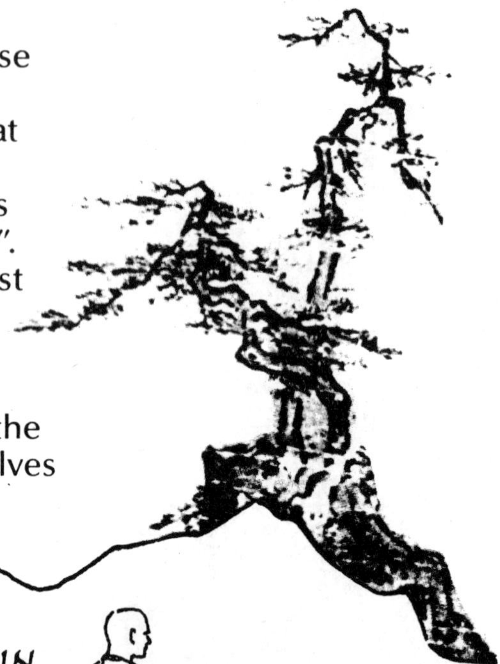

the MAN SEES the MOUNTAIN
the MOUNTAIN SEES the MAN

Beginner's mind is unified mind. It is being completely involved in whatever we are doing. The great Master Obaku used to bow so much in his Zen practice that he always had a big lump on his forehead, so he really knew about bowing. He said:

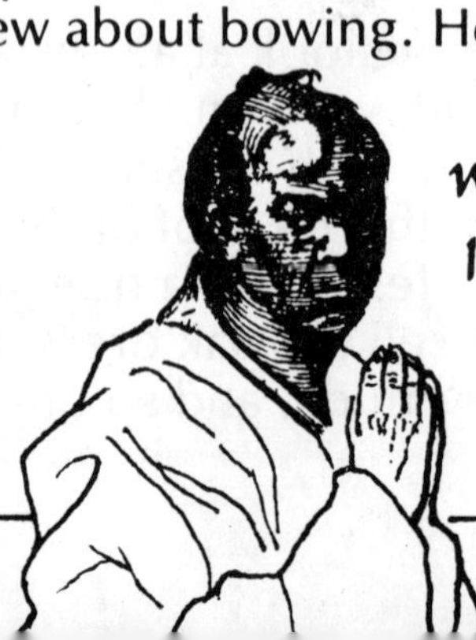

WHEN I BOW,
I JUST BOW.

Zen practice is for people who don't mind always being at the beginning, because every moment is new, which mean that we are new, because we are not separate from the moment. The Zen masters say that we should experience our lives as if for the first time, without any of our old fears and prejudices. If we can forget to protect our separate selves and let life in completely, we can have a really good time.

EARLY HISTORY

The word Zen is the Japanese translation of the Sanskrit word dhyana, which means meditation. Rather than observing numerous rules and studying holy scriptures, Zen Buddhists emphasize meditation as the path to enlightenment.

This is not to say that some practitioners do not observe rules and read books. Some say that there are more books about Zen than about any other form of Buddhism.

Common to all Buddhist sects is the reliance on the unbroken transmission of Buddha's teachings from teacher to student. In this way, the original understanding has been continuously passed down for the last twenty-five centuries. Zen sects place a lot of importance on this authenticity; they all trace themselves back to Buddha. So we will start with him.

BUDDHA

The historic data about Buddha's life do not completely agree. From sect to sect, his birth is placed anywhere from 983BC to 440BC. We will take the most accepted version and say that he was born in the 6th century BC and died in the 5th century BC. From here on, this is the common legend.

BUDDHA?! NOT YET. I'M PRINCE GAUTAMA!

Buddha was born a prince into the royal family of the Sakya clan.

The state his father ruled was situated on the slopes of the Himalayas on what today is the border of Nepal and India. Somewhat removed from the power wars between the other states in the valley of the Gangesh River, it enjoyed relative peace and prosperity. When Prince Gautama (that was Buddha's name) was born, there were many auspicious signs. One that worried his father was the prophecy of an old sage that Gautama would become a great holy man. Determined to have a successor to the throne, he surrounded the young prince with all the luxuries of palace life, and forbade him ever to leave the royal grounds.

Then finally, one day, he took his first excursion outside the palace. As he was being driven in his royal chariot, he encountered an old woman. Surprised at the sight, he asked his driver what had happened to her. He was told that everyone eventually gets old and feeble.

Continuing the ride, he came next to a sick person. To the prince's amazement, he was informed that everyone is subject to sickness. Then they drove past a procession carrying a corpse.

Gautama was deeply shocked to hear that every living being dies. While still immersed in this disturbing revelation of sickness, old age and death, his chariot came upon an old man whose eyes were glowing and who gently smiled at him.

The prince made a firm decision to attain liberation. One night he left the palace, his wife and son, and became a wandering ascetic. He became an arduous practitioner of all kinds of austerities, but somehow he felt he wasn't getting anywhere.

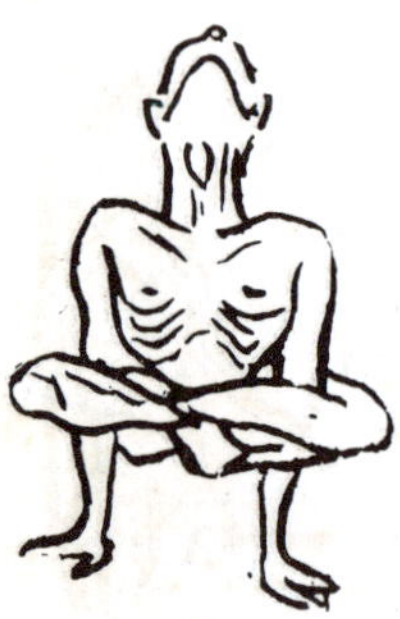

After one of his long fasts, he broke the rule of the ascetics and accepted some rice cooked in milk from a village woman.

Then, with great determination, he sat on his straw mat underneath a Bodhi tree and vowed not to move until he had seen ultimate reality. Gautama spent seven days in meditative absorption. On the morning of the seventh day he opened his eyes and saw the morning star. In that instant, he attained enlightenment.

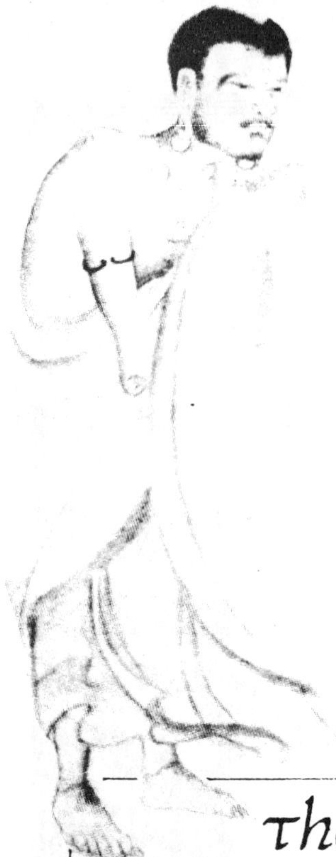

For a while he questioned whether he should teach or spend the rest of his life in seclusion. Then he came upon five of his ascetic friends. At first they shunned him because he had broken the ascetic rule, but when they saw the beautiful light shining from his face, they followed him. That day, Buddha gave his first discourse in a place called the Deer Park. The Buddha Tathagata, as he will be known from now on, meaning "the awakened one, who has gone completely through," talked about the Four Noble Truths, which became the foundation of Buddhism. They are:

THE FOUR NOBLE TRUTHS

1. LIFE IS SUFFERING
2. SUFFERING IS CAUSED BY SELFISH CRAVING
3. SELFISH CRAVING CAN BE OVERCOME
4. THE EIGHTFOLD PATH
   TO OVERCOMING SELFISH CRAVING:
   - RIGHT UNDERSTANDING
   - RIGHT PURPOSE
   - RIGHT SPEECH
   - RIGHT CONDUCT
   - RIGHT LIVELIHOOD
   - RIGHT EFFORT
   - RIGHT ALERTNESS
   - RIGHT CONCENTRATION

We won't go here into the details of Buddha's later life, except to mention the incident which all schools of Zen consider to be the origin of the unique Zen viewpoint.

This is the story in which the Tathagata gave the direct mind to mind transmission of ultimate reality to one of his disciples.

One day a large gathering was assembled on Vulture Peak and Buddha was expected to give a talk. Instead, he sat silently for a long time, and then lifted a flower, without saying a word. Everyone was dumbfounded. Only old Mahakasyapa smiled. He had experienced the great awakening.

Mahakasyapa became Buddha's successor.

At the age of eighty, Buddha died. His last words were,

He left no written teaching. After his death, his disciples reconstructed his discourses and the story of his life from memory. Much of the Buddhist scripture dates from centuries later, and is usually considered to be the record of teachings that were passed down orally from generation to generation.

During his life, Buddha ordained many monks and nuns into a life of seclusion and contemplation, and this solitary mode of practice became widespread in the subsequent centuries, reaching out into Southeast Asia and China.

In general, liberation was defined as the perception of the emptiness or nonsubstantiality of persons. Monks and nuns would analyse their bodies and minds and see them as composites of numerous transitory and interdependent phenomena. They would conclude that a person is not a self-sufficient entity and does not exist as the controller of the body and mind.

This insight would provide them with a basis for detachment from the world. The goal of this detachment was Nirvana, a mental condition of unperturbed peace.

Around 100 AD, a new interpretation of Buddhism emerged, which emphasized compassion. Its ideal was not a solitary life, but the path of the bodhisattva, the devotion of one's entire life to helping others. The bodhisattva vows to sacrifice even his or her liberation until all sentient beings are free from suffering. This new interpretation was called Mahyana, or the Great Vehicle, while the old way came to be called Hinayana, or the Lesser Vehicle.

NAGARJUNA

The founder of Mahayana Buddhism was the great philosopher, Nagarjuna. He claimed that nothing affirmative or definitive could be said about ultimate reality. In this way, he tried to uproot the tendency to cling, however subtly, to the notion that the ultimate is an entity or a state existing in itself, separate from concrete experience. Thus, the understanding of emptiness was stretched to include both persons and phenomena.

BODHIDHARMA

This Mahayana viewpoint was the basis of the new style of teaching which Bodhidharma, the First Patriarch of Chinese Zen (or Chan) Buddhism (and the 28th Patriarch of Indian Buddhism) brought to China from India. Many historians believe that Bodhidharma himself never existed, and that the lives of many teachers were combined into one for the purpose of tracing the source of various Zen lineages. But the legend is that he came from Ceylon to China around 520 A.D. At that time, Mahayana Buddhism was already established in China. There were many universities where one could study Buddhist psychology and philosophy. It was Bodhidharma's insistence on meditation practice and the direct insight into the truth which caused the revolution in Chinese Buddhism and gave birth to Zen.

Upon Bodhidharma's arrival in China, he went to see Emperor Wu, who was a generous patron of Buddhism, and a Mahayana practitioner himself. The Emperor said to Bodhidharma,
I have built many monasteries and universities. Please tell me, what merit have I earned?
NONE WHATSOEVER.
The Emperor was astonished.
And what is the meaning of the sacred truth?
Limitlessly open, nothing is sacred!
Then tell me, who are you?
I don't know,
came Bodhidharma's now famous answer.

At this the Emperor was completely confused. Bodhidharma left, crossed the Yellow River to the state of Wei, where he sat in meditation for nine years facing a wall. The time was not right for his teaching.

One day, a monk came to visit him. It was Kuang, later to become Hui-ke, the Second Patriarch of Zen Buddhism. He implored Bodhidharma to be his teacher, but the First Patriarch ignored him. It was a bitter winter, and Kuang stood outside waiting, until he was knee deep in snow. Bodhidharma was still not convinced of his earnestness.

In despair, Kuang took his sword and cut off his right arm, and presented it to Bodhidharma. He begged for teaching,

After this encounter, Bodhidharma assumed the role of teacher.

He spent his life at the Shao-lin Monastery, where he is credited with the invention of the martial art, Kung-fu.

Towards the end of his life, he decided to return to India. He called his closest disciples before him to test their understanding. The first was Tao-fu.

Second was the nun, Tsung-chih.
As I understand, it is seen once and never again.
You have my flesh.
Third was Tao-yu.
Empty are the four elements and non-existent the five skandhas. According to my view, there is not a thing to be grasped as real.
You have my bones.
Finally Hui-ke bowed reverently to his master, and then stood before him silently.
And you have my marrow.

HUI-KE

Hui-ke now became the Second Patriarch, and Bodhidharma left for India. He was quite old by then, some accounts say over one hundred and fifty years.

TAOISM

During the time of the Third Patriarch, Seng-ts'an, Zen was strongly influenced by Taoism, a spiritual tradition, indigenous to Chinese soil, which had already flourished there for almost a thousand years. Based on the teaching of Lao-tzu, a contemporary of Buddha, Taoism emphasized the non-interference with the natural order of reality, which, he claimed, functions spontaneously.

LAO-TZU

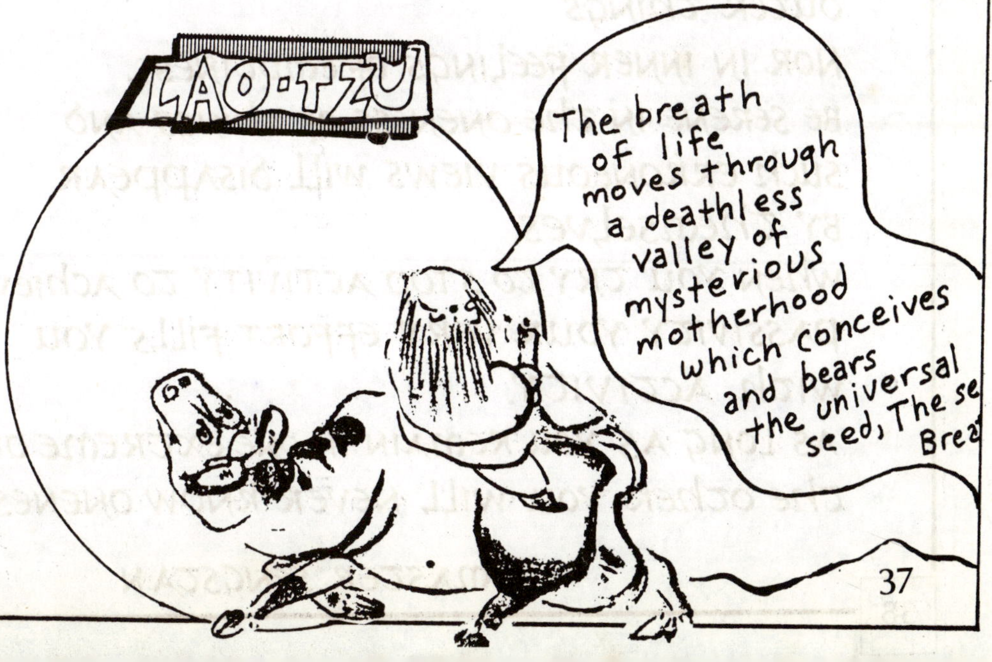

SENGSTAN

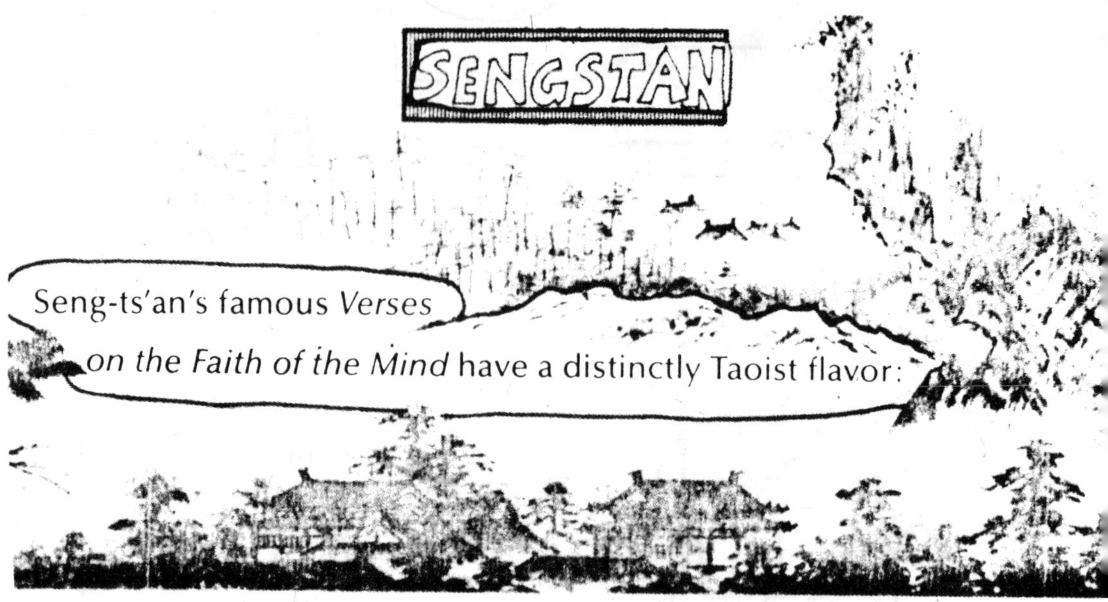

The way is perfect like vast space
where nothing is lacking and nothing
is in excess.
Indeed, it is due to our choosing to
accept or reject that we do not see the
true nature of things.
Live neither in the entanglements of
outer things
nor in inner feelings of emptiness.
Be serene in the oneness of things and
such erroneous views will disappear
by themselves.
When you try to stop activity to achieve
passivity your very effort fills you
with activity.
As long as you remain in one extreme or
the other you will never know oneness.

Master Sengstan

Zen did not become recognized as a distinct sect of Buddhism until the Sixth Patriarch, Hui-neng (638-713 AD). His appearance and style fully embodied the spirit of Zen and he began the period which became known as the Golden Age of Zen.

HUI-NENG

Hui-neng grew up in the undeveloped south of China. He was quite poor and supported himself and his mother by selling fire wood. One day, in the street, he heard a monk reciting the Buddhist "Diamond Sutra." He experienced a deep awakening and decided to find a teacher.

Having somehow provided for his mother, he traveled to northern China to Master Hung-jen, the Fifth Patriarch of Zen and abbot of a large monastery with five hundred monks.

When he arrived, the master tested him by expressing the common prejudice of the time,

SOUTHERN MONKIES HAVE NO BUDDHA-NATURE. HOW DO YOU EXPECT TO ATTAIN BUDDHAHOOD?

Young Hui-neng replied,

THERE MAY BE SOUTHERNERS AND NORTHERNERS, BUT IN THE BUDDHA NATURE THERE ARE NO DISTINCTIONS.

The master was impressed, but could not allow the illiterate peasant to join the other monks, so he gave him menial labor as a rice pounder.

About eight months had passed when the Fifth Patriarch decided to look for a successor. He announced a contest, asking everyone to express his understanding in a short poem and post it on a wall of the monastery. Since all of the monks expected the oldest and most learned among them, Shen-hsiu, to win, his was the only poem to appear on the wall. It read,

THE BODY IS LIKE A BODHI TREE,
AND THE MIND A MIRROR BRIGHT,
CAREFULLY WE WIPE THEM
EVERY DAY
AND LET NO DUST ALIGHT.

This poem expressed the style of meditating prevalent at that time. Thoughts and conflicting emotions were seen as a pollution of the mind, which, when prevented from arising would leave the mind clear to reflect reality as it is. Thus, mental quiescence was the primary goal for monks and nuns. Hui-neng, hearing about the contest, asked a monk to read him the posted poem and then to write out his answer (Hui-neng was illiterate, although he was said to quote many sutras eloquently). Hui-neng's poem went like this,

THE BODY IS NOT LIKE A BODHI TREE,
AND THERE IS NO MIRROR BRIGHT,
SINCE EVERYTHING IS EMPTY
TO BEGIN WITH,
WHERE CAN THE DUST ALIGHT?

Hui-neng had understood emptiness. His poem asserted that there can be no distinction made between phenomena, like thoughts and emotions, and the mind-awareness which reflects them. All the monks wondered who had dared to post this second poem, but the Patriarch knew that there was only one man at the monastery with this depth of understanding.

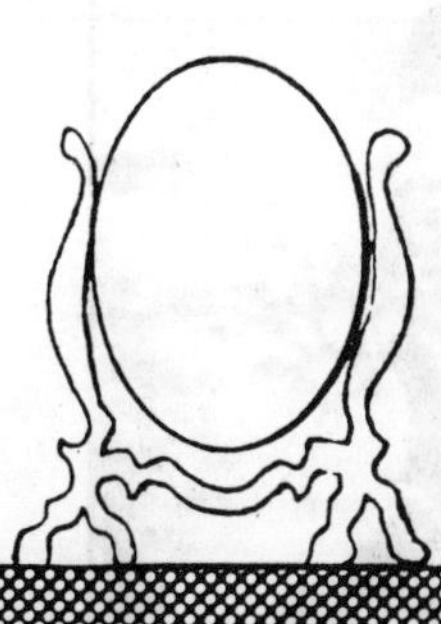

One night, when everyone was asleep, he called Hui-neng to his room and presented to him the robe and the bowl of the Patriarchs.

Fearing the jealous rage of the other monks, he advised Hui-neng to run away and hide in the mountains.

SO HUI-NENG FLED.

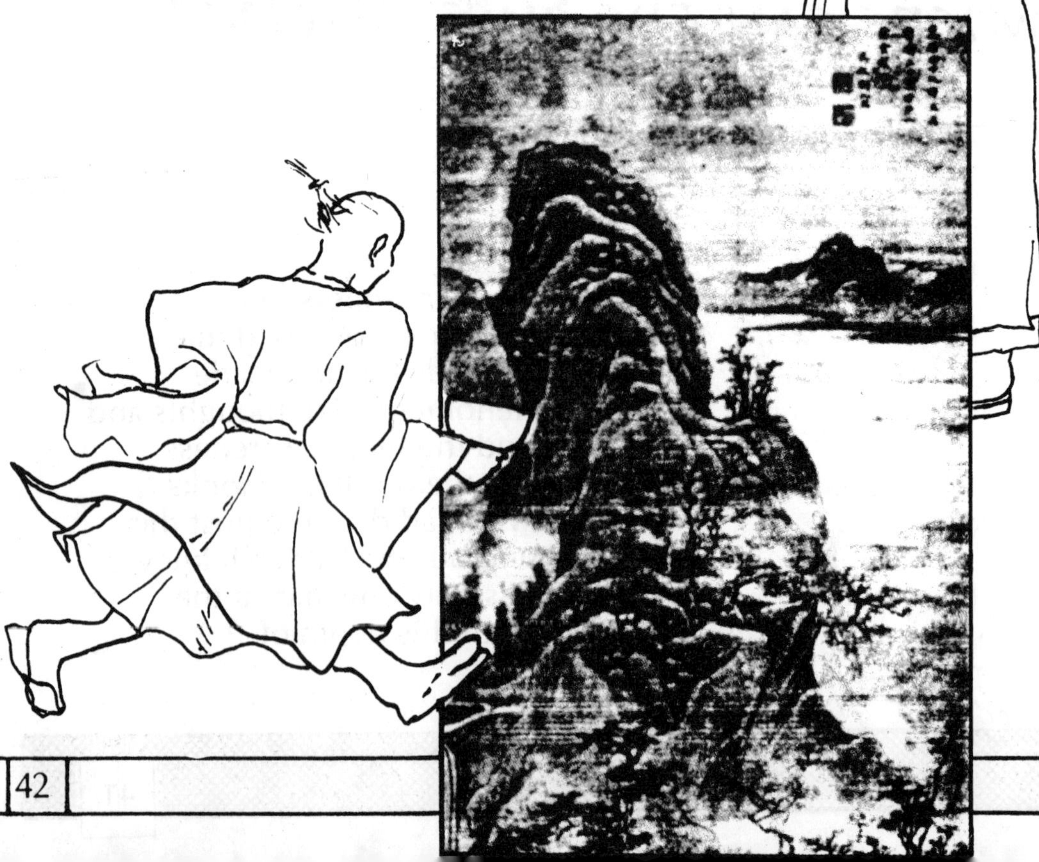

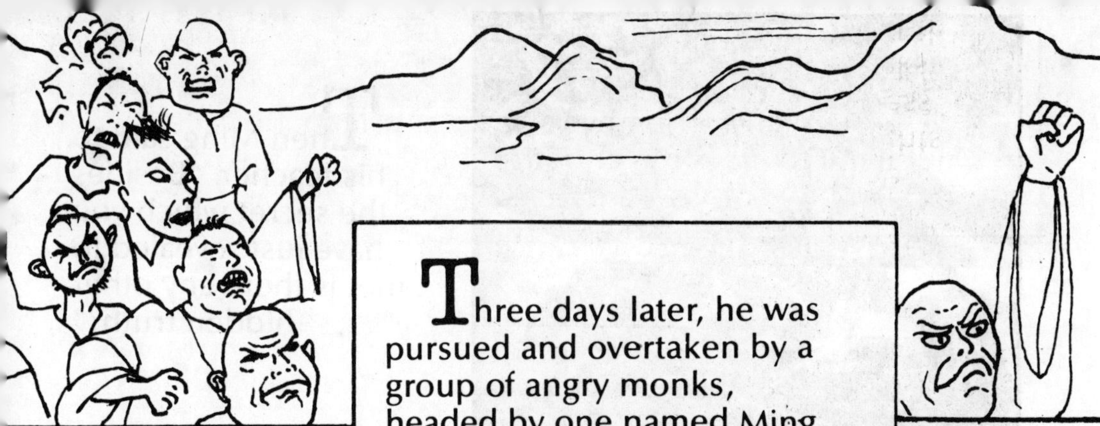

Three days later, he was pursued and overtaken by a group of angry monks, headed by one named Ming.

Hui-neng put the robe and bowl on a rock and said to Ming,

This robe symbolizes our patriarchal faith and it should not be taken by force. You may take it if you wish.

Ming tried to take it from the rock, but to his amazement, he was unable to lift it. Trembling, he said to Hui-neng, "I have not come for the robe and bowl. Please teach me." Hui-neng said,

If you have come for teaching, think not of good and evil. At this moment, what is your original face, which you had even before your birth?

Instantly, years of practice came to fruition for Ming and he attained enlightenment.

Then Ming said to his teacher, "Besides the secret which you have just revealed to me, is there any other hidden truth?"

Hui-neng answered, "In what I have just revealed, there is nothing hidden. If you look within yourself and find your true face, then the secret is in you."

Hui-neng spent the next ten years living in the seclusion of the mountains. During that time, the Fifth Patriarch died, transmitting the lineage to Shen-hsiu as well. In 676, at the age of thirty-nine, Hui-neng began his public career as a teacher. He came first to the Fa-hsing temple. Entering the gates, he heard two monks, arguing near the flagpole.

One said, "The flag is moving." The other said, "The wind is moving." The Sixth Patriarch said,

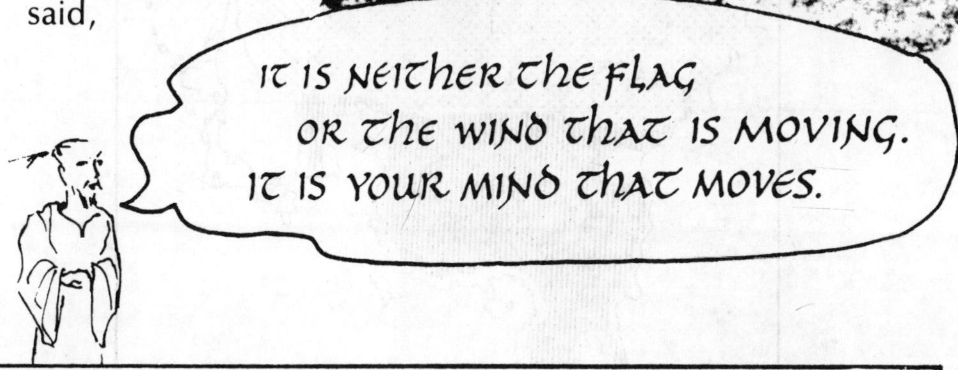

The abbot of this temple then called Hui-neng and asked for the Zen teaching.

China

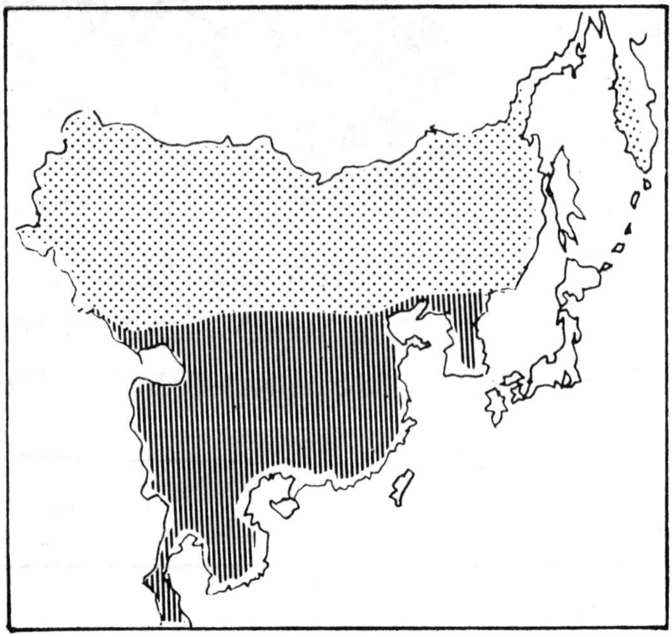

Gradual Enlightenment

Sudden Enlightenment

Hui-neng traveled to the south where he spent most of his life teaching at the Pao-lin Monastery. Breaking with the tradition of using Sanskrit (Indian) terminology, his sayings spring entirely from his Chinese background and gave Zen its characteristic tone. His style became known as the "sudden enlightenment" or Southern School of Zen, in contrast to the "gradual enlightenment" or Northern School whose Sixth Patriarch was Shen-hsiu.

Hui-neng is credited with the rase, "seeing into one's own nature", hich is one of the best known and ost used Zen lines. He emphasized is seeing, which is an instantaneous ent, over the gradual process of velopment. His "Platform Sutra" says,

hen the abrupt doctrine
is understood there is no need
of disciplining oneself in
external things.
If one always has the right view
within one's mind,
one will never be deceived.
This is seeing into one's own nature.

At that time, there was quite a dispute between the followers of the Northern and Southern Schools. Although Hui-neng and Shen-hsiu were friendly towards each other, it is said that some monks of the Northern School attempted an unsuccessful assassination of Hui-neng.

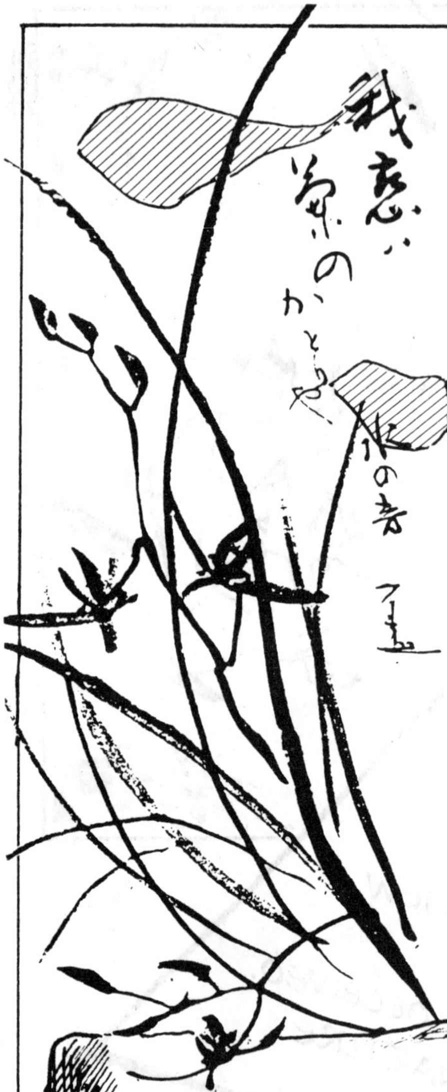

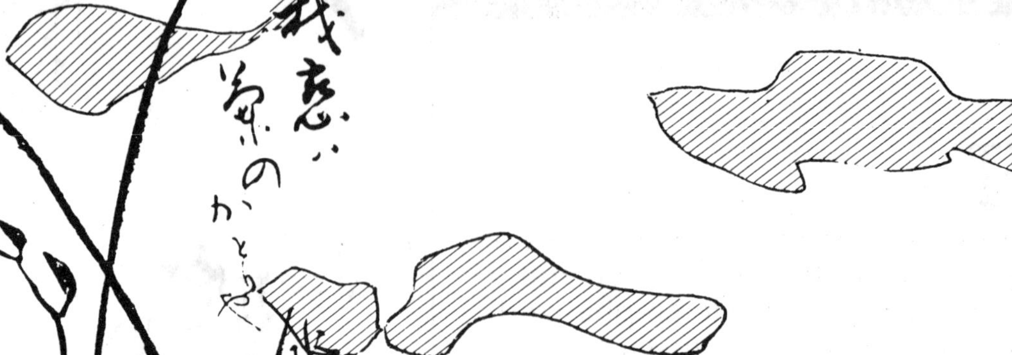

Hui-neng died at the age of seventy-six during the peak of Chinese culture under the Tang Dynasty. He had several thousand disciples who spread the teaching of his sudden enlightenment school. More than a hundred years after his death, Tsung-yuan, one of China's greatest writers, inscribed this on his tombstone:

ACCORDING TO HIS DOCTRINE, NON-DOING IS REALITY, EMPTINESS IS THE TRUTH, AND THE ULTIMATE MEANING OF THINGS IS VAST AND IMMOVABLE. HE TAUGHT THAT HUMAN NATURE, IN ITS BEGINNINGS AS WELL AS IN THE END, IS THOROUGHLY GOOD AND DOES NOT REQUIRE ANY ARTIFICIAL WEEDING-OUT, FOR IT HAS ITS ROOTS IN THAT WHICH IS SERENE.

ZEN PRINCIPLES

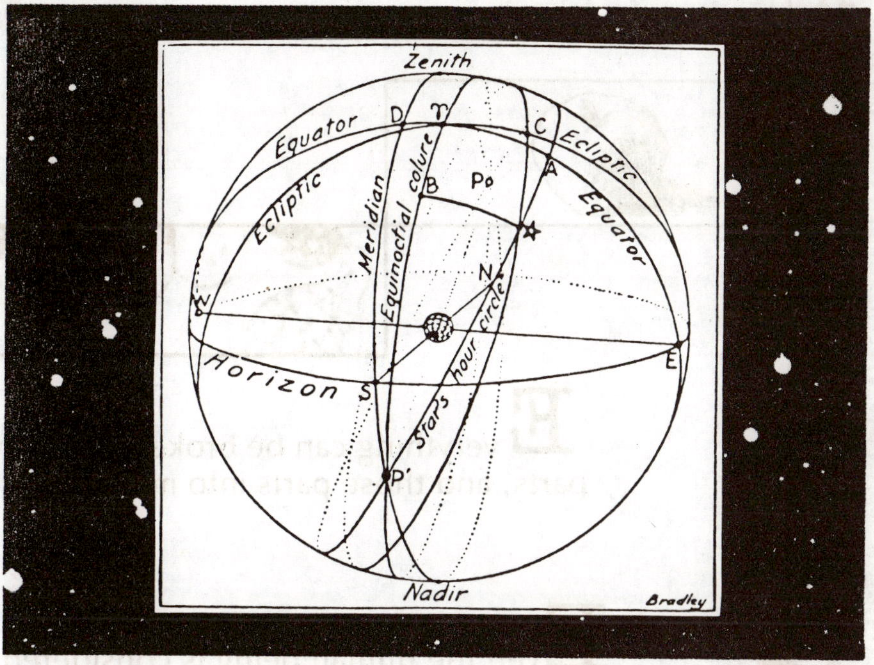

Zen Buddhists believe that the universe is a single, dynamic interdependent whole, and that the more distinctly we become ourselves, the more we realize that we each exist only in relation to this whole. Buddhism calls this interdependent condition "emptiness". Everything is caused by something, and in turn, is cause for something else.

And nothing exists eternally.

Everything in the universe is subject to decay.

And nothing exists essentially.

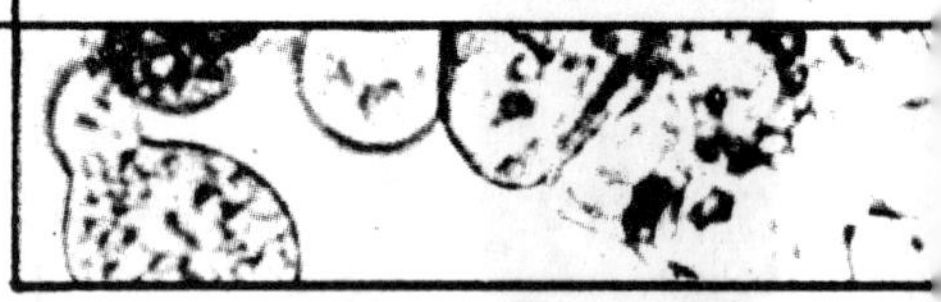

Everything can be broken down into parts, and those parts into more parts.

Even the human being is considered to be a constantly changing interplay of physical elements and psychological tendencies. Enlightenment in Zen is often called the "great death," meaning the death of these psychological patterns it calls the ego. As the ego dissolves, the perception of duality between subject and object also dissolves.

One of the most subtle and most important points to understand in Zen doctrine is described in the line from the Heart Sutra "form is emptiness, emptiness is form."

FORM IS EMPTINESS, EMPTINESS IS FORM

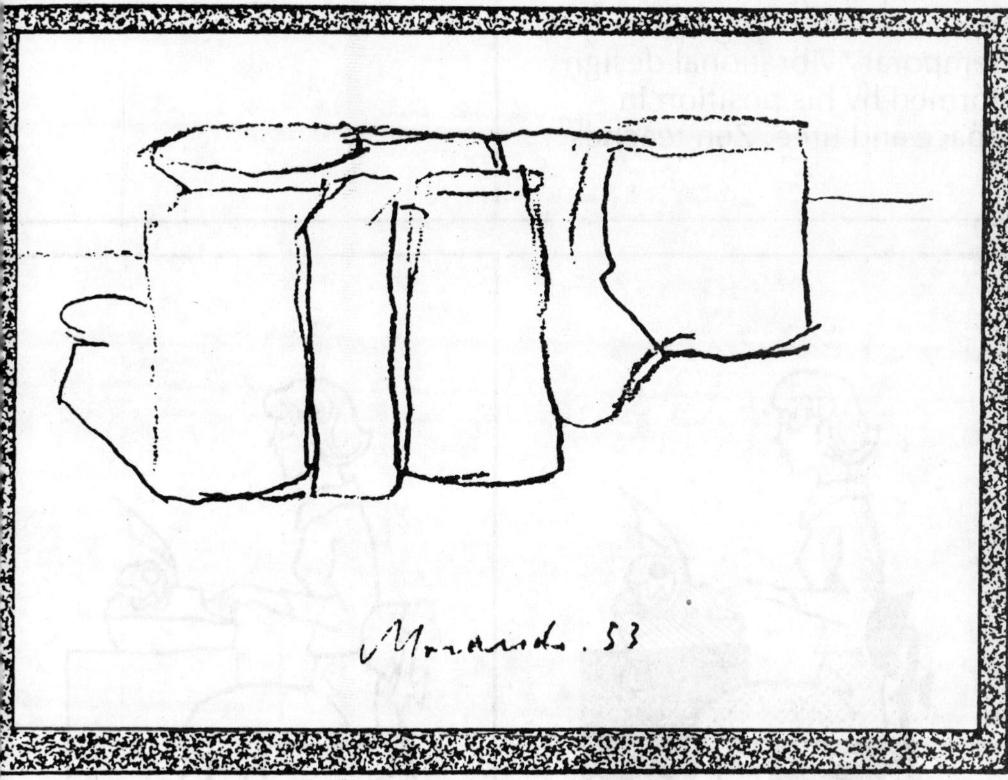

Emptiness is not to be understood as something separate from or beyond our actual universe. It is the relative nature of all forms in the universe, in other words relativity itself, which is the emptiness of these forms.

So a chair is a chair and it is also not a chair (although we can choose to call that particular pattern of atoms at that particular moment by the word chair) and a human being is certainly a human being (for example, he will react if pinched), but he is also not a human being but only a temporary vibrational design formed by his position in space and time. Zen teaches that our suffering begins when we impose upon this fluid, interdependent moment of experience the illusion of independent selfhood, and then attempt to protect this false selfhood from losing those imposed boundaries to the forces which surround it.

Zen says that all conflict arises from the illusion of multiplicity in a world which is actually completely unified and continuous. True enlightenment is the equal recognition of the oneness of all forms and of the uniqueness of each form. It is both complete realization and fulfilment of one's individual life and the realization that one has no separate existence, that one is the "ten thousand things" of the universe. A contemporary Zen master says that one must fully develop negative energy (no self) and positive energy (complete self) to attain the zero of perfect enlightenment. So while our ego is dying, our sensation and our knowledge of ourself is all the time becoming more vivid.

"O Brethen, the Mind-Reality has no definite form. It permeates and runs through the whole universe. In the eye it acts as sight; in the ear it acts as hearing; in the nose it acts as the sense of smell; in the mouth it speaks; in the hand it grasps; in the feet it walks. All these activities are originally but one single spiritual illumination, which diversifies itself into harmonious correspondences. It is because the Mind has no definite form of its own that it can so freely act in every form." *Master Rinzai*

Some Zen teachers have described the univers as one mind which expresses itself in many different forms. They say that when someone is enlightened his/her own individual mind reaches thi fundamental level of the one mind.

The Buddhist principle that nothing exists independently or eternally has often been misunderstood.

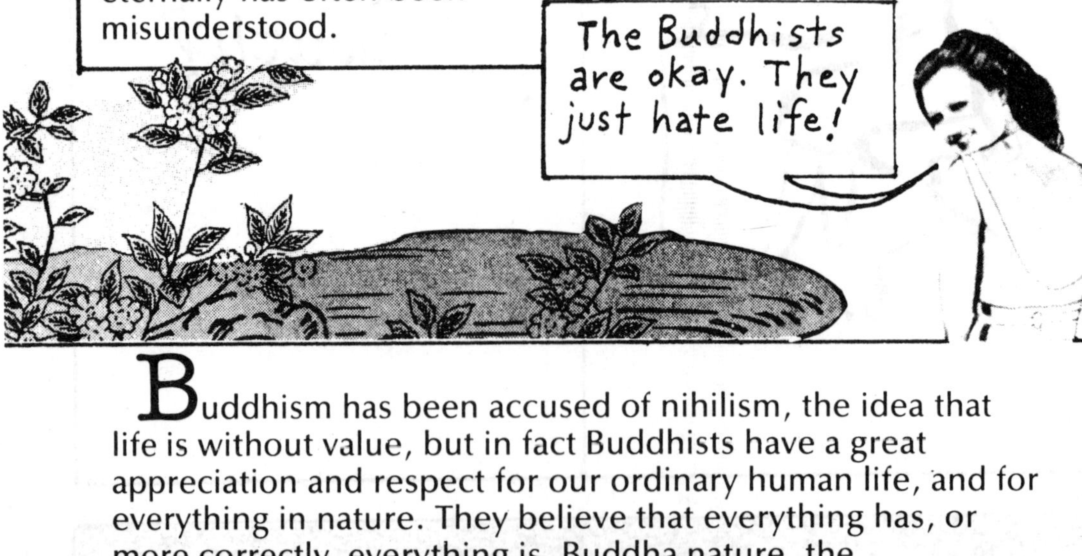

Buddhism has been accused of nihilism, the idea that life is without value, but in fact Buddhists have a great appreciation and respect for our ordinary human life, and for everything in nature. They believe that everything has, or more correctly, everything is, Buddha nature, the manifestation of the one mind.

This is why, when Bodhidharma, the First Patriarch of Zen was asked by the Chinese Emperor Wu, "What is the primary meaning of the sacred truth?", Bodhidharma said, "Limitlessly open, nothing is sacred." He could just have well have said that everything is sacred.

LIMITLESSLY OPEN, NOTHING IS SACRED!

Zen masters emphasize that the enlightened mind is just our ordinary mind, and that when we are most spontaneous, most honestly ourselves, then we are closest to utimate reality. Zen almost always describes ultimate reality in terms of our everyday, concrete reality. For example:

Once a monk went to see Master Tung-shan (Jap. Tozan), who was busy weighing flax. The monk asked

WHAT IS BUDDHA-NATURE?

The master immediately answered,

THREE POUNDS OF FLAX

They say that the difference between an ordinary person and an enlightened person is that to an ordinary person, experience is concrete, but an enlightened person is always aware that life is both empty and concrete.

Po-chang Huai-hai
(Jap. Hyakujō) wrote:

Wisdom here means the ability to distinguish every sort of good and evil; dhyana (zazen) means that, though making these distinctions, you remain wholly unaffected by love or aversion.

Zen teaches that the relative and the absolute interpenetrate each other everywhere in the universe, that is, every moment of our lives belongs to this oneness. The 9th century Zen master Hsuah-Feng (Jap. Seppo) said:

It is said that when the Buddha attained his enlightenment under the bo tree, he exclaimed in amazement that all beings are inherently enlightened, we just don't know it. He taught that it is only our own confusion which veils from us our natural wisdom and goodness.

Here is how a twentieth century Zen master put it:

YOUR MIND CAN BE COMPARED TO A MIRROR which REFLECTS EVERYTHING THAT APPEARS BEFORE IT. FROM THE TIME YOU BEGIN TO THINK, TO FEEL, AND TO EXERT YOUR WILL, SHADOWS ARE CAST upon your mind which distort its reflections. This condition we call delusion, which is the fundamental sickness of human beings.

The most serious effect of this sickness is that it creates a sense of duality, in consequence of which you postulate "I" and "not-I". The truth is that everything is one, and this of course is not a numerical one. Falsely seeing oneself confronted by a world of separate existences, this is what creates antagonism, greed, and, inevitably, suffering.

The purpose of zazen is to wipe away from the mind these shadows of defilements so that we can intimately experience our solidarity with all life. Love and compassion then naturally and spontaneously flow forth

Buddhism teaches that we project our own fantasies onto our real circumstances. Real circumstances become clear to us only after we attain enlightenment. Until then, we may regard life as a dream, as the conjuring of our imagination, from which, hopefully, we will one day awake.

Human distortion of reality, the Buddhists say, arises from three main habits:

That is, by denying or manipulating any irritating situation, we sabotage the fullness of our experience. As one contemporary Zen master said, "Zen is the completion of meaning." The fullness of our experience, this meaning, is beyond conceptual interpretation.

"ZEN IS THE COMPLETION OF MEANING"

Buddhists believe that our lives unfold according to a natural law of cause and effect which they call the law of karma. This means that our circumstances are the result of our past actions, and even our thoughts. So even though life flows as automatically as a river flows or as the seasons change, our future is always shaped by the way we choose to act in the present. The more we can see through our greed, anger and ignorance, the more satisfying are our circumstances.

HEAVEN AND HELL

SO YOU HAVE A SWORD. IT'S PROBABLY TOO DULL TO CUT OFF MY HEAD.
HERE OPEN THE GATES OF HELL.
HERE OPEN THE GATES OF HEAVEN

Zen is very practical. It's not a philosophy—in fact, most of its teaching is aimed at getting us to shift our focus from abstract understanding to a more thorough experience with our whole mind. This includes every level of sensation, emotion, intuition, and reason at one time.

the traditional description of Zen attributed to Bodhidharma is:

a special transmission
outside the scriptures
no dependence
on words and letters
direct pointing
to the real person
seeing into one's nature
and attainment of Buddhahood.

Zen teachers are always trying to free their students from the trap of intellectual analysis and to deepen their actual living experience. Here's a story on this theme:

One day, four traveling monks came to visit Master Hogen. They asked if they might build a fire in his yard to warm themselves. While they were building the fire, Hogen heard them discussing subjectivity and objectivity. He joined them and said,

HERE IS A BIG STONE. DO YOU CONSIDER IT TO BE INSIDE OR OUTSIDE OF YOUR MIND?

One of the monks replied,

...observed Hogen.

This story also shows that when you are enlightened, you realize that there is no inside or outside of the mind.

ZEN PRACTICE

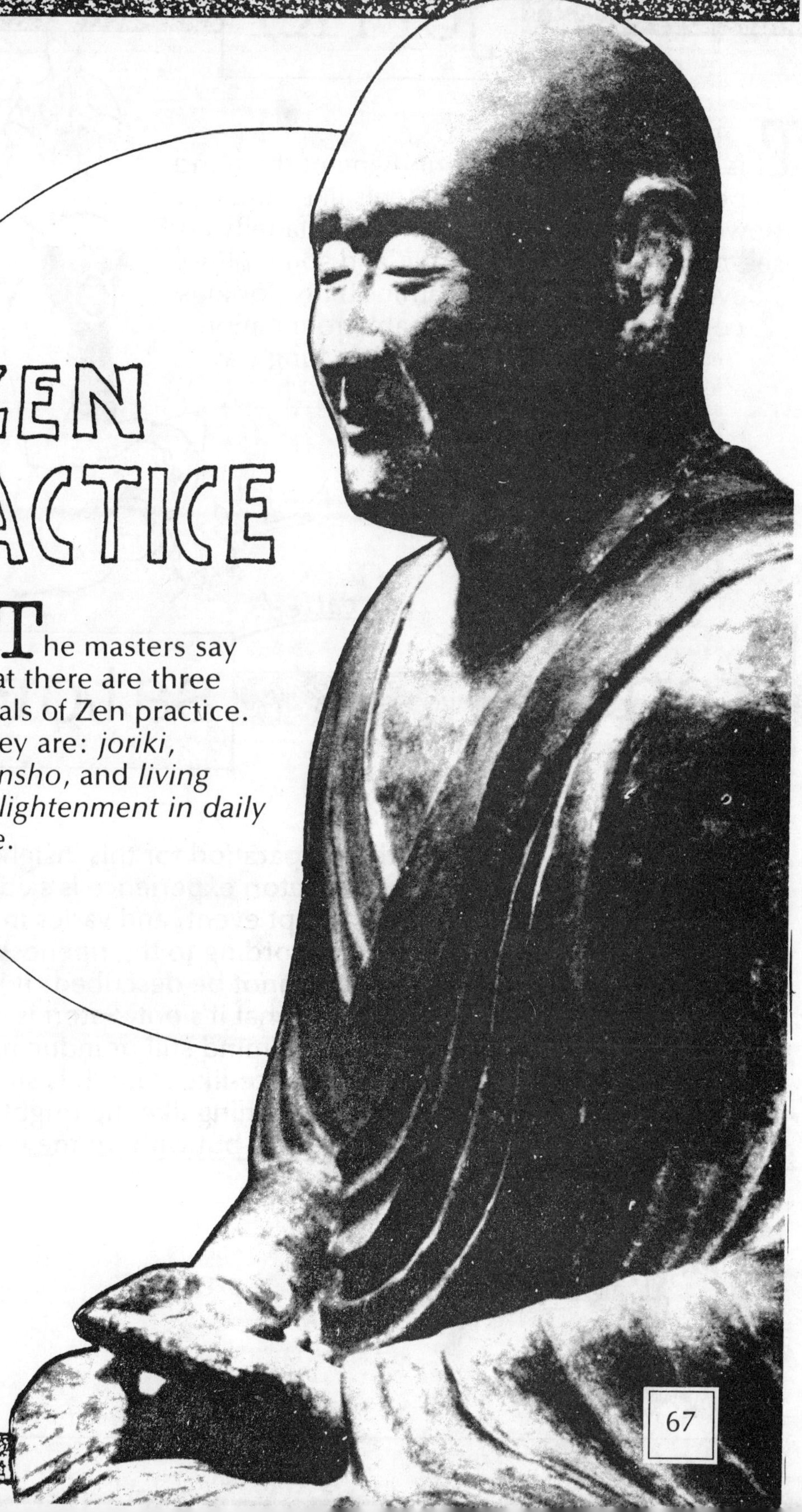

The masters say that there are three goals of Zen practice. They are: *joriki*, *kensho*, and *living enlightenment in daily life*.

joriki

This is the balancing and unifying of the mind. A person with lots of joriki feels like, and is, a powerful mass of energy. Both spontaneity and self-control come from joriki, and some people develop healing or telepathic ability. Joriki is considered the indispensable foundation of Zen practice, but by itself, a long way from enlightenment.

also called:

kensho satori

Although the preparation for this insight is gradual, the actual Satori experience is said to be a sudden and abrupt event, and varies in its depth of clarity according to the ripeness of the student. Satori cannot be described; it is a little easier to say what it's not. Satori is not forcibly holding the mind still or inducing a hypnotic or trance-like state. It is super alertness. It is something like the brightest idea you can have, but without the idea.

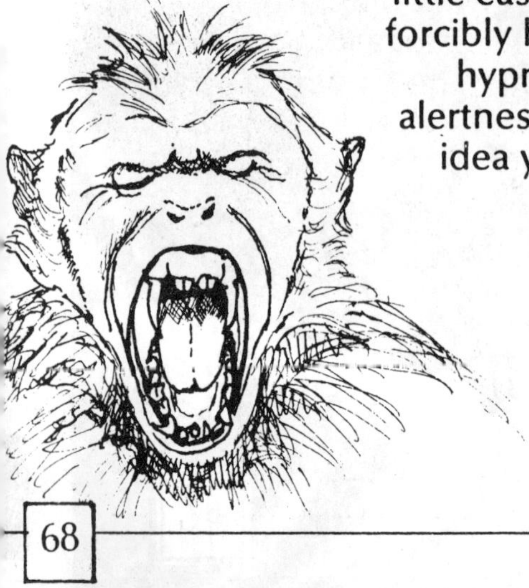

Satori is not a product of the intellect. It involves the wisdom of our whole body-feeling-mind organism. That wisdom is always there. In Satori, whatever illusions have been veiling it from our direct perception suddenly fall away. Hui-neng said: "In original nature itself there is wisdom and because of this, self-knowledge. Nature reflects itself in itself, which is self-illumination not to be expressed in words."

The moment of Satori has come to people, usually after years of work, in many different ways: during meditation practice, or in daily life, triggered by some vivid sight or sound, or in dialogue with a Zen master, such as in the famous anecdote in which:

A student said to the master, "I feel as though I have been raising a goose in a bottle. Now the goose is so big that I can't get it out without either breaking the bottle or harming the goose." The master said to the student, "Sir, it's out!". Hearing this, the student instantly awakened to reality.

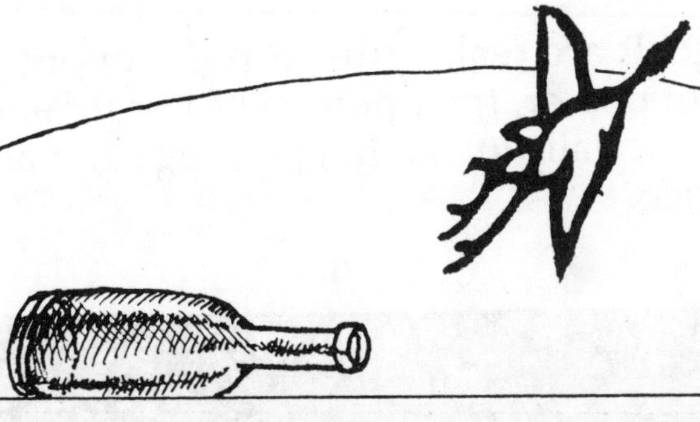

Living Zen in Daily Life

These three goals are really three aspects of one goal–the accumulation of power, the opening of insight and the transformation of our daily life all happen together as the result of Zen practice.

zazen

Probably most Zen practitioners would agree that the most important part of their practice is meditation, called zazen. Zazen is usually done sitting on a cushion with the back straight and the legs crossed. The right hand is held about two inches under the navel with the palm upward, the left hand rests in the right, also palm upward, and the tips of the thumbs are touching. The eyes are half closed with the gaze relaxed, focused neither inward or outward.

Attention is focused just below the navel (called the Hara), which relaxes the body and steadies the mind, making it easier to stop the habitual babble in our heads (in India, they say that the mind is like a mad monkey).

THE OLD ZEN MASTERS SAY THAT WE SHOULD SIT WITH NOBLE STRENGTH LIKE A GREAT PINE TREE OR AN IRON MOUNTAIN.

The 4 Basic Techniques of zazen

1- COUNTING THE BREATHS

This meditation is usually given to a beginning student. Either the inhale or the exhale is counted from one to ten. If any thought other than the count arises, you have to stop wherever you are and go back to one.

For example—
inhale, exhale, one
inhale, exhale, two
inhale, exhale, wow, I've actually stopped thinking, damn . . .
inhale, exhale, one
and so on, sometimes for several years, until the "mad monkey" finally settles down.

SOME TEACHERS SAY THAT THE THOUGHTS THEMSELVES ARE NOT A PROBLEM. IT IS POSSIBLE TO LET THE THOUGHTS COME AND GO WITHOUT GETTING DISTRACTED BY THEM. HUI-NENG CALLED THIS STEADY ATTENTION "NON-ABIDING MIND", MEANING THAT THE MIND NEVER GETS STUCK ANYWHERE. SO IT IS SOMETIMES TAUGHT THAT AS LONG AS YOU CAN COUNT FROM 1 TO 10 BREATHS WITHOUT LOOSING TRACK YOU CAN KEEP GOING.

2- FOLLOWING THE BREATHS

This is a slightly more advanced practice. The student is now instructed to remain constantly aware of the breath without counting. In zazen, the breath is always allowed to follow its natural rhythm, but as the practice progresses, it automatically becomes slower and deeper and more even.

This produces a very pleasant sensation of lightness in the body and clarity in the mind.

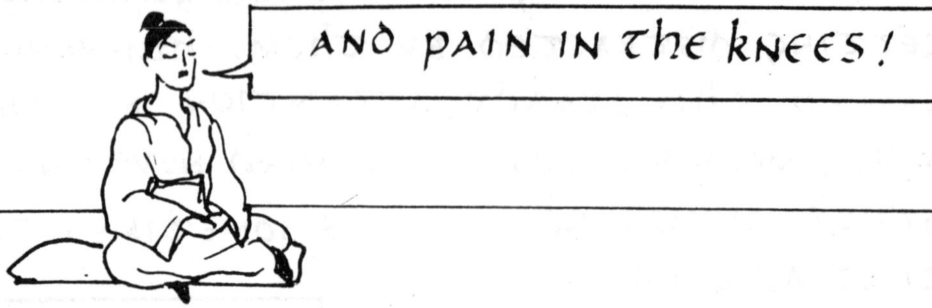

3-SHIKAN-TAZA

This is sometimes said to be the most difficult, most advanced type of zazen. It is just simply sitting without any object of concentration. Sometimes it is begun by imagining oneself to be in a 360 degree sphere of awareness, but even that image must eventually be given up. Shikan-taza is often compared to the alertness of someone involved in a life or death sword fight. Most important is to sit in the faith that this "just sitting" can and does naturally unfold to total self-realization, called Buddhahood.

4-KOANS

Koan is a style of practice so uniquely Zen that the two are almost synonyms. The main task for a Zen teacher is to awaken the student to the presence of the Absolute.

At the moment the student is ready to actually open his eyes to the truth, the master would not hesitate to use any word, shout, or even deliver a blow to push the student over the edge.

Koans are the documents of these interactions between masters and students. The emphasis of the koan is always on the ultimate question, which can be stated as :

"WHO AM I ?"

OR:

"WHAT IS THE ABSOLUTE?"

It is said that there are three essential qualities which enable one to solve the koan:

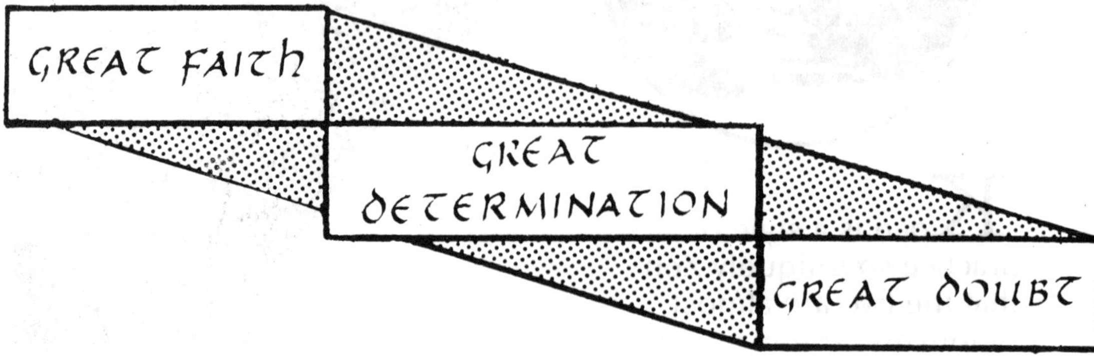

Probably the most famous of all Zen koans is Joshu's Mu:

A monk asked Master Joshu, DOES A DOG HAVE BUDDHA-NATURE?

Joshu answered, MU!

The monk was immediately enlightened.

Here are Master Mumon's famous words of advice for people working on Mu:

concentrate your whole self, with its
60 bones and joints and 84,000 pores,
nto mu making your whole body a solid
ump of doubt. day and night, without
easing, keep digging into it. but don't
ake it as "nothingness" or as "being"
r as "non-being".

it must be like a red-hot iron ball
which you have gulped down and
hich you try to vomit up, but cannot.

you must extinguish all delusive
houghts and feelings you have
p to the present cherished.

AFTER A CERTAIN PERIOD OF SUCH EFFORTS MU WILL COME TO FRUITION, AND INSIDE AND OUT WILL BECOME ONE NATURALLY. YOU WILL THEN BE LIKE A DUMB MAN WHO HAS HAD A DREAM AND THEN AWAKENS. YOU WILL KNOW YOURSELF AND FOR YOURSELF ONLY.

THEN ALL OF A SUDDEN, MU WILL BREAK OPEN AND ASTONISH THE HEAVENS AND SHAKE THE EARTH.

It is said that Master Mumon himself worked on the koan Mu for six years. Finally, one day, upon hearing the monastery drum, he realized the Great Enlightenment.

Koans are grouped into five categories which represent progressive stages of enlightenment:

DHARMAKAYA OR HOSSHIN koans are devised to give the student a first insight into ultimate reality.

KIKAN koans further differentiate between real and unreal experience.

GONSEN koans penetrate the words of the Patriarchs.

NANTO or "difficult to pass through" koans dissolve dualistic notions of having attained enlightenment.

FIVE RANKS are the peak of formal practice of koans. Through them one may realize the spontaneous unity of Absolute and Relative.

MASTER HAKUIN WROTE, REGARDING THE TONE AND PROCESS OF KOAN WORK:

... IT IS LIKE A MAN WHO IS SEEKING FISH. HE MUST FIRST OF ALL LOOK IN THE WATER. FISH ARE A PRODUCT OF THE WATER; OUTSIDE THE WATER THERE ARE NO FISH.

JUST SO, YOU WHO WISH TO SEEK BUDDHA MUST FIRST OF ALL LOOK INTO YOUR OWN MIND. BUDDHA IS A PRODUCT OF THE MIND; OUTSIDE THE MIND THERE IS NO BUDDHA.

Once the koan practice is completed, the student proceeds to an examination of the ten precepts, which he or she vowed to keep when first formally entering into Zen training. The precepts can now be seen from an enlightened perspective as the spontaneous manifestation of one's true nature.

10 Precepts:

Not destroying life

Not stealing

Not committing unchaste acts

Not lying

- Not taking intoxicants
- Not speaking of others' faults
- Not slandering others by praising yourself
- Not coveting
- Not being angry
- Not insulting the Three Treasures (the Buddha, his teachings, the Zen community).

Ma-tsu's comment summarizes the Zen attitude towards the precepts: The master was asked, "What about eating meat and drinking wine?" He answered, "Eating meat and drinking wine are your natural birthright, but by doing so, you are missing your chance for greater blessedness."

zendo

Of course, zazen can be practiced at home, but many people prefer to sit formally in a monastery or zendo (meditation room). Formal Zen practice is quite formal, aiming to subdue the student's willful ego and habitual desires for comfort and escape. The precision required in the various Zen rituals develops harmony in the mind and body, and unifies the student's concentration. The description given below is only one version of Zen training, each school does it a little differently.

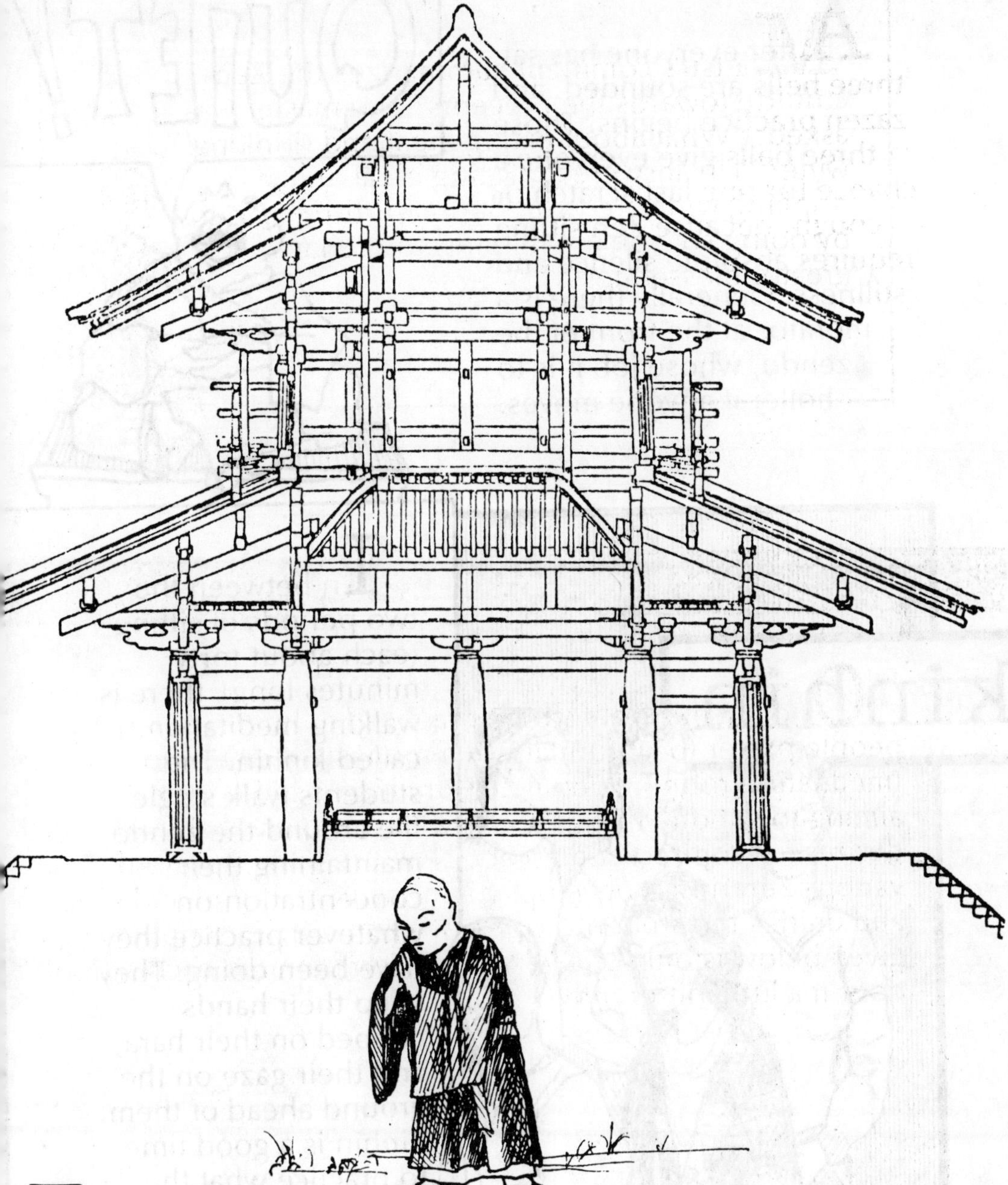

Entering the zendo, the student bows, placing the palms of the hands together. In Japanese Zen, this is called gassho. Then there is another bow in front of one's cushion. First you bow towards the cushion, representing your respect for your true self, and even your not so true self for getting to the zendo (it's usually about 5:30 in the morning at this point; then there's another sitting in the evening), and then you bow away from the cushion towards your fellow students (affectionately called Zennies).

After everyone has sat, three bells are sounded, and zazen practice begins. Those three bells give everyone a chance for one last scratch or cough, because Zen sitting requires absolute silence and stillness. Generally there is a monitor at the front of the zendo, whose job it is to holler if anyone moves.

kinhin

In between the two periods of sitting (each about forty minutes long), there is walking meditation, called kinhin. The students walk single file around the zendo, maintaining their concentration on whatever practice they have been doing. They keep their hands cupped on their hara, and their gaze on the ground ahead of them. Kinhin is a good time to practice what the Zen masters call, "keeping the feet warm and the head cool."

roshi

During the sitting, the students can go for interview with the teacher (called Roshi). The teacher-student relationship is considered very important in Zen. On entering the interview room, the student bows at the door and again in front of the teacher, then sits down in front of her or him (eyeball to eyeball) to be thoroughly psyched out, encouraged, scolded, advised, ignored or possibly hit with a wooden stick, depending on what is needed at that moment to further the student's realization. If you've had, or think you've had, kensho, your experience must be validated by the teacher, who will probably know the minute you walk in the room, and who can give you certain "test questions" which reveal the depth of your understanding.

kyosaku

Also during the sitting, at most zendos, either the teacher or a monitor will walk around the room carrying a wooden stick called a kyosaku. In some monasteries, the monitor will surprise, if not shock, a sitter by hitting him or her from behind without warning. In others, students ask to be hit by placing the palms together in gassho. Then the monitor also bows and delivers a swift, carefully aimed blow to each of the student's shoulders. Then both the student and the monitor bow again. It helps if they've both seen the movie in which Mifune strolls serenely down the road with several arrows stuck in his back. Why would anyone ask to be hit? The kyosaku actually benefits zazen practice in several ways. It is a relief, after sitting motionless for a long time, to get some circulation going in the shoulders. It is an excellent cure for sleepiness. And nothing disrupts an engrossing daydream quite like a whack with a wooden stick. Some people have even experienced satori when a timely kyosaku penetrated their last bit of resistance. It is said that to be effective, the kyosaku must be wielded with a mixture of compassion, power and wisdom. However, it is also said that in some monasteries in Japan, if a monitor breaks a kyosaku on someone's shoulders, he (the monitor!) is rewarded with a bottle of sake.

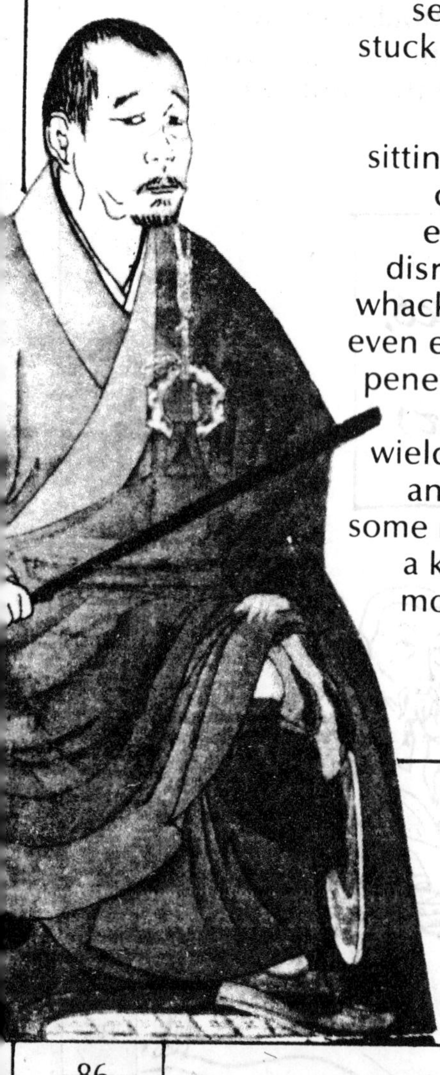

chants

At the end of the two periods of sitting, there is the chanting of the Four Vows:

> Sentient beings
> are numberless.
> I vow to save them.
> Desires
> are inexhaustible.
> I vow to put an end
> to them.
> The dharmas
> are boundless.
> I vow to master them.
> The Buddha way
> is insurpassable.
> I vow to attain it.

MAHAYANA

The Great Vehicle

The vow to save all other sentient beings, even before you save yourself, distinguishes Mahayana Buddhism (the great vehicle) from Hinayana Buddhism (the lesser vehicle). Zen came out of Mahayana Buddhism. Compassion towards all forms of life is considered to be inseparable from enlightenment, the experience of the fundamental oneness of the universe.

makyo

Some people go through a phase of practice in which they begin to have visions or other kinds of hallucinations. This is not at all considered to be an exalted state in Zen. It is called Makyo, the product of the subconscious mind which has been stirred by intensive zazen. One is advised to recognize its illusory nature, and then ignore it. In a deeper sense, any of our ideas or images which prevent us from seeing ultimate reality are called makyo.

drums & bells

After sitting is over in the evening, a series of drums and bells are played and this encouraging message is recited by the monitor:

LET ME RESPECTFULLY REMIND YOU,
LIFE AND DEATH ARE OF
SUPREME IMPORTANCE.
TIME PASSES SWIFLY AND
OPPORTUNITY IS LOST.
EACH OF US MUST STRIVE
TO AWAKEN, AWAKEN.
TAKE HEED. DO NOT SQUANDER YOUR LIVES.

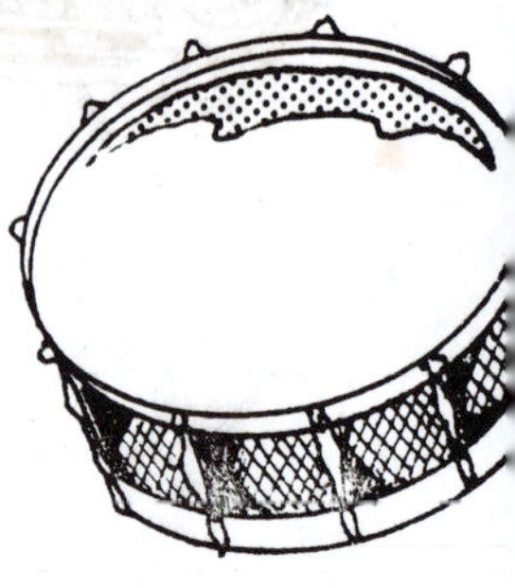

work

Work, usually manual labor, is traditionally an important part of Zen practice. People living in monasteries clean the buildings, cultivate the grounds and wash an inordinate number of dishes as part of their daily activity. (The cooking is usually done by someone advanced in his or her practice, and "Cook" is a very respected position.) The tradition of hard labor probably started when Zen was emerging in China. Those entering a monastic life did not pay taxes, so tough work was necessary to fend off tax evaders. But, also, it was, and is, an excellent way to subdue an overactive intellect and to develop virtues like humility and endurance.

The man credited with establishing "work practice" in the Zen schedule is Po-chang Huai-hai, an 8th century Zen master who coined the phrase, "a day without work is a day without food." Today Po-Chang might be called a workaholic. When he had grown quite old, his students became worried that he would make himself sick by working so much and contrived to hide his garden tools. No problem, the old master simply stopped eating until his tools were returned to him.

sesshin

One week out of every month, there is an intensive called sesshin. Zazen is increased to nine or ten hours a day, meals are taken formally in the zendo, students are not allowed to talk or to look around at each other, and intellectual activities like reading and writing are also forbidden. The Roshi gives a talk every day of the sesshin in which some koan or other aspect of Zen practice is discussed.

In some monasteries in China and Japan, sitting continues even through the night. The monks are provided with "chin rests," which is a very refreshing way to sleep, especially for the chin.

jukai

Jukai is a ceremony which officially marks a person's entrance onto the path of Zen Buddhism. The student is usually given a dharma name by the teacher, and a rakasu, a rectangular piece of cloth which hangs from a band around the neck. In some schools, the students sew their own rakasus, chanting the mantra Namu Dai Butsu (I am one with the great Buddha) with every stitch. The new Zen Buddhists vow to obey the precepts and to become one with the Three Treasures. There are also ceremonies for becoming monks or nuns, and for receiving the transmission, in which one becomes a roshi with the authority to teach the Buddha dharma.

religion??

Zen may be the only religion which encourages the student to outgrow religion. Although Zen training demands enormous dedication, reverence and discipline, once a student has attained enlightenment, and that realization has been confirmed by the teacher, he or she is expected to have "seen through" the outer forms of rules and rituals. It does not matter then if one remains in the monastery or goes off alone as long as one is free of attachment to all images, even images of the Buddha. The very famous 9th century Master Rinzai said, "I look for the one who stands alone." And a contemporary Roshi says, "I am waiting for the moment that I can push you off the cliff and you can climb back up by yourself." Master Rinzai said that all the Buddhist teachings are "expedient means, temporary remedies for curing diseases." All forms even the most respected, are relative and temporary.

"IF YOU MEET THE BUDDHA, KILL HIM"– BUT NOT UNTIL YOU MEET HIM!

LATER HISTORY

Here we are back in China. It is the 8th century and the golden age of Zen has begun. The followers of Hui-neng's sudden enlightenment style have multiplied like mushrooms after the rain. Everyone is trying hard to find new ways to induce a sudden breakthrough into the enlightened state of mind.

The most prominent figures in this group are Ma-tsu (709–788) and Shih-tou (700–790).

Shih-tou

Ma-tsu

Ma-tsu was the inventor of almost all famous "hard" Zen methods. Punches, kicks, and even beatings, and deafening shouts were his most favorite.

His contemporary, Shih-tou, was quite the opposite. He preferred gentleness.

Both became a decisive influence in the course of Zen's history; Ma-tsu's descendants founded two, and Shih-tou's three of the five "houses" or sects that Zen had at its peak. Together, they produced an all-star bunch of Zen masters. It is remembered that Ma-tsu alone had one hundred and thirty-nine enlightened disciples.

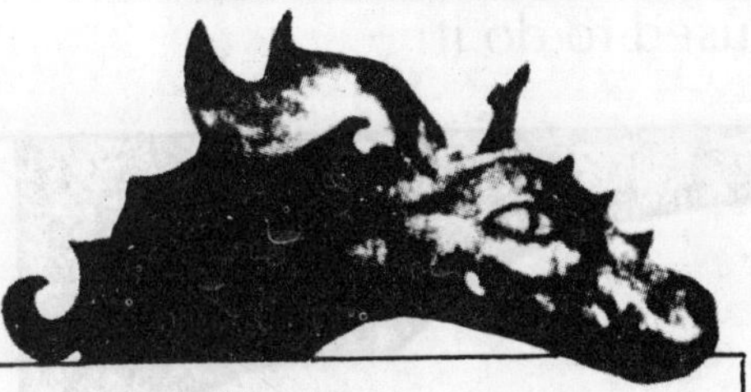

Ma-tsu
(Baso, in Japanese)

Nan-ch'uan
(Nansen)

Chao-chou
(Joshu)

Po-chang Huai-hai
(Hyakujō)

Huang-po
(Obaku)

Lin-chi
(Rinzai)

Shih-t'ou
(Sekito, in Japanese)

Tung-shan
(Tozan)

Ts'ao-shan
(Sozan)

Dogen

There was a saying at the time: "In Kiangsi, the master is Ma-tsu; in Hunan the master is Shih-tou. People go back and forth between the two and those who never meet either master are completely ignorant."

The two styles of Zen existing today, the Rinzai and the Soto, are basically the styles of Ma-tsu and Shih-tou respectively.

Ma-tsu felt that since the original mind is inherent in everyone, all that was necessary was to awaken the student to its presence. Here is how he used to do it:

A monk asked Ma-tsu for the primary meaning of Zen.

Ma-tsu knocked him down to the ground, saying, "If I don't strike you, the whole country will laugh at me."

The monk was enlightened on the spot.

Once Master Ma-tsu was lying on the road with his legs outstretched. A monk came by pushing a cart and requested that he draw back his legs so that he could pass.

••• replied the monk and pushed the cart over the master's legs.

Ma-tsu returned to the monastery hall, grabbed an axe and yelled, "let the one who injured me come forward." Without hesitation, the monk came forward and exposed his neck. An approving Ma-tsu put down the axe.

Not all of his interactions with his students were violent. In this next story, Ma-tsu was sitting with three of his disciples, and asked, "What should we do right now?" One monk answered, "We should study the sutra." The second mond said, "It would be better to do some meditation." Then the monk Nan-ch'uan (Jap. Nansen) got up, shook the sleeves of his robes, and walked away. Ma-tsu said,

Eventually Nan-ch'uan got the transmission from Ma-tsu (also called the mind seal) and went off to become a famous Zen master. He stayed for thirty years in the monastery which he built himself in the Anhwei province of Northern China. Some say that he never went out of the monastery in all those years. There are many recorded interactions between him and his most famous disciple, Chao-chou (Jap. Joshu). Although probably the most brilliant team in Zen history, their line ended quickly with Chao-chou who never found a successor.

When Chao-chou was still a novice, e approached Master Nan-ch'uan and sked,

"WHAT IS THE WAY?"

"ORDINARY MIND IS THE WAY."

"HOW SHOULD I PURSUE IT?"

asked Chao-chou. And Nan-ch'uan said:

"IF YOU MOVE TOWARDS IT, IT MOVES AWAY."

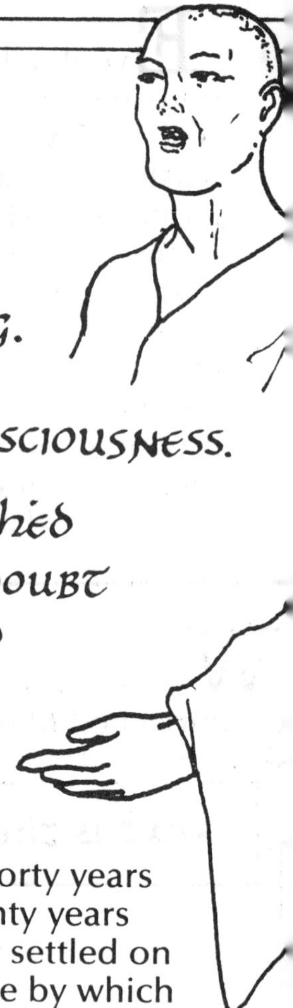

then how can I attain knowledge of it?"

"The way does not belong to knowing or not-knowing. Knowing is delusion; not-knowing is blank consciousness.

When you have really reached the true way beyond all doubt you will find it as vast and boundless as outer space."

Chao-chou stayed with Nan-ch'uan for forty years until Nan-ch'uan's death. He then spent twenty years freely wandering across China until he finally settled on Mt. Chao-chou (in Japanese, Joshu), the name by which he is remembered today. During this time, his fame spread far and wide. Here are some anecdotes from his teaching career:

One day he fell down in the snow and cried out, "Help me up, help me up!" A monk ran over and lay down beside him. Chao-chou got up and walked away.

(If you can guess who learned what in the above situation, you are doing better than the authors).

Once a monk begged Chao-chou to tell him the most important principle in Zen. Chao-chou excused himself, saying,

"I have to go now and make water. Just think, even such a trifling thing, I have to do in person."

Chao-chou stayed for forty years on his mountain. He died there at age 120, leaving no successors.

PO-CHANG HUAI-HUAI

Ma-tsu's line was continued by Po-chang Huai-hai. Huai-hai is credited with the invention of monastic Zen. By uniting the monastic rules of both Hinayana and Mahayana Buddhism, he set a firm foundation which has enabled Zen to continue until the present day.

He introduced obligatory work, a smart political move at a time when there was growing resentment towards the tax-exempt Buddhist monks and nuns. He rejected begging as their primary means of support and attempted to make the monasteries self-sufficient. He was a prolific writer on Zen teachings.

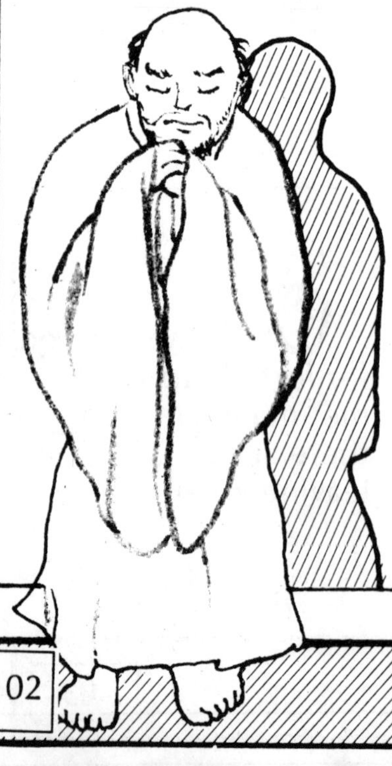

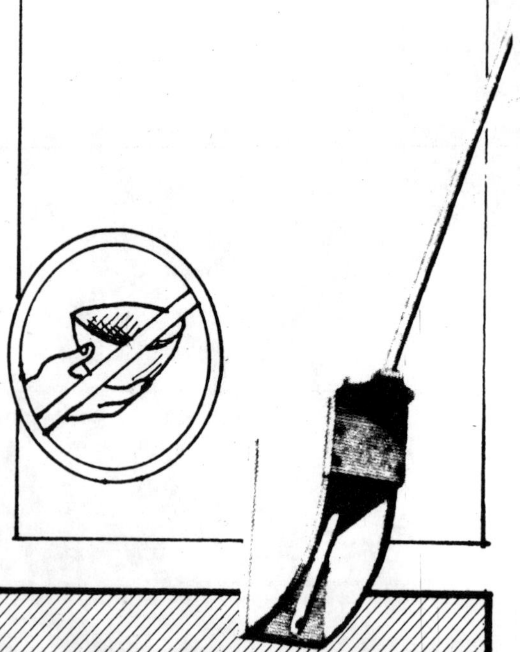

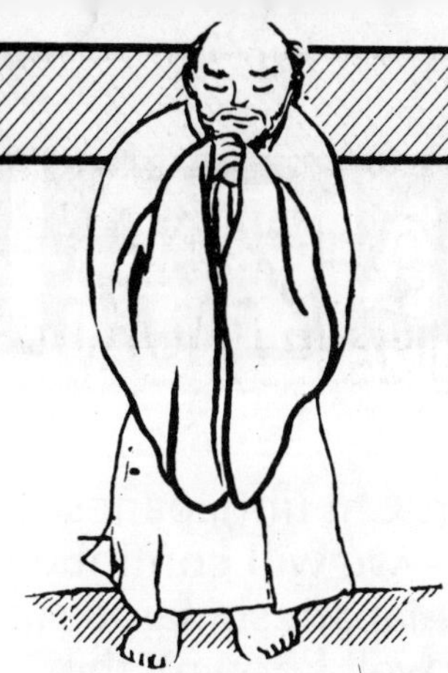

Here is an example of his writings:

THE NATURE OF THE ABSOLUTE IS VOID AND YET NOT VOID. HOW SO? THE MARVELOUS "SUBSTANCE" OF THE ABSOLUTE, HAVING NEITHER FORM NOR SHAPE, IS THEREFORE UNDISCOVERABLE; HENCE IT IS VOID. NEVERTHELESS, THAT IMMATERIAL, FORMLESS "SUBSTANCE" CONTAINS FUNCTIONS AS NUMEROUS AS THE SANDS OF THE GANGES, FUNCTIONS WHICH RESPOND UNFAILINGLY TO CIRCUMSTANCES, SO IT IS ALSO DESCRIBED AS NOT VOID.

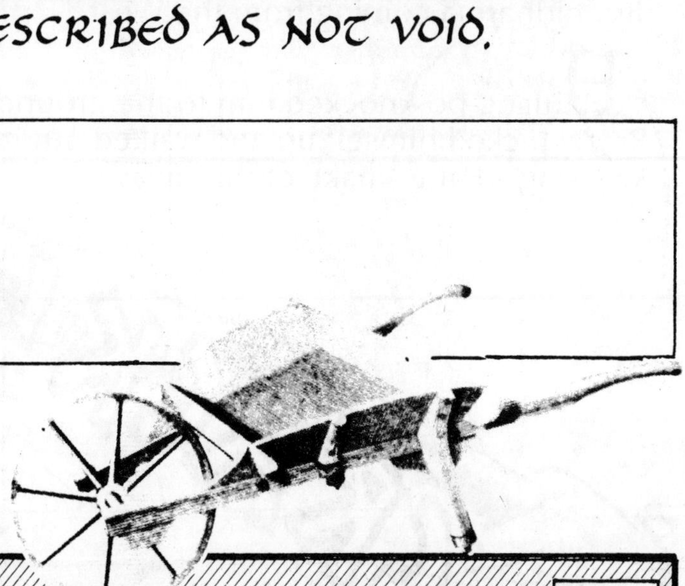

RINZAI

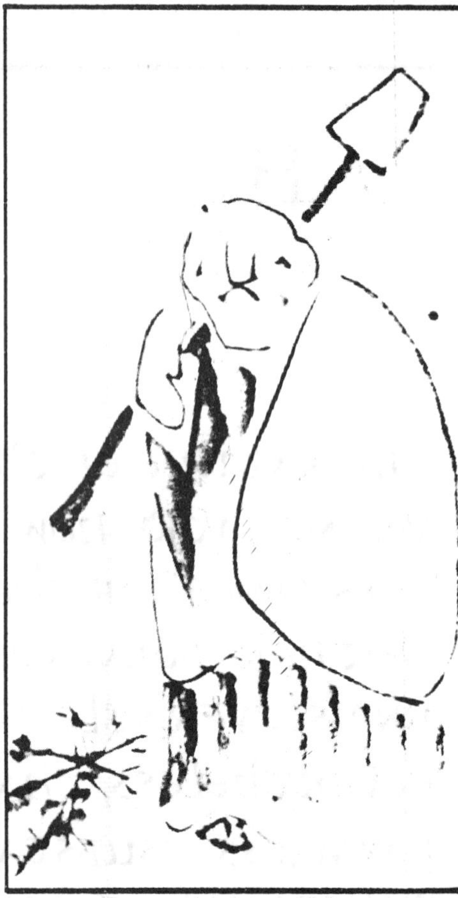

Lin-Chi (in Japanese, Rinzai—we will continue to use his Japanese name since it is so well known), the founder of the Rinzai sect, was a descendant of Master Huai-hai. He was a very wild fellow, as we can see from the description of his first enlightenment experience. Rinzai studied with Master Huang-po (Huai-hai's successor) for three years but was not satisfied with his own progress.

The head monk suggested that he go to see the master himself. So Rinzai went to Huang-po and asked the standard question, "What is the meaning of Bodhidharma coming from the West?"

Huang-po knocked him to the ground with his stick. Rinzai picked himself up and walked out in confusion, not knowing what to make of this answer.

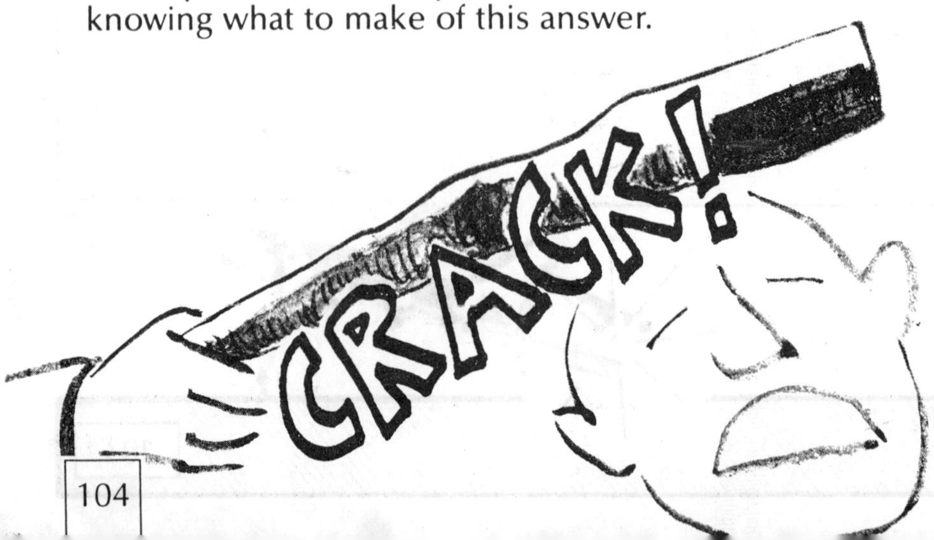

The head monk advised him to try again. He did, twice more, but the answer was the same. Demoralized, he announced that he was leaving the monastery. Huang-po then directed him to a neighboring Zen teacher named Ta-yu. When Rinzai related his experience with Huang-po to Ta-yu, Ta-yu's comment was, "How compassionate Huang-po is. He was just trying to relieve you of distress." Hearing this, Rinzai suddenly had a deep awakening to his original nature. He could not contain himself. He jumped up and down, exclaiming, "Huang-po's Zen is very simple, there's nothing to it!"

"You scamp," said Ta-yu, "a minute ago you said that Huang-po's Zen was impossible to understand, now you say there's nothing to it. What have you realized? Speak at once!" At this, Rinzai punched Ta-yu in the ribs three times. Ta-yu kicked him out, saying, "Your teacher is Huang-po, so you are no concern of mine."

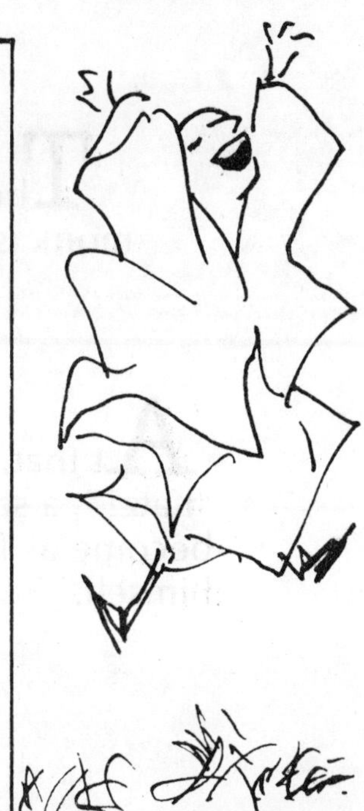

Rinzai went right back to Huang-po who greeted him at the gate with,

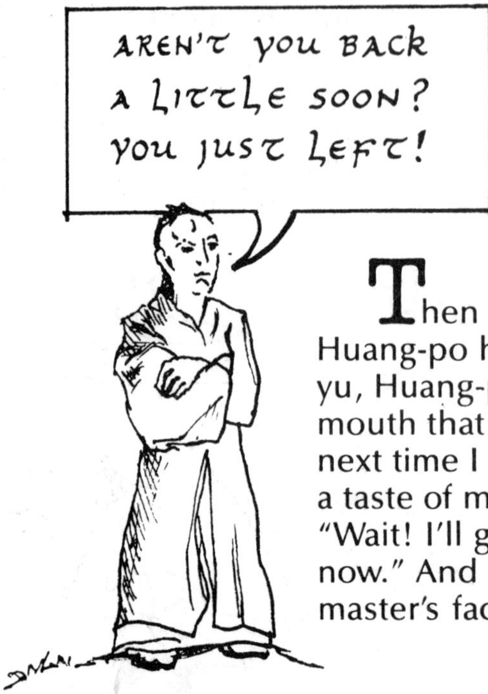

Rinzai bowed deeply and said,

Then Rinzai related to Huang-po his encounter with Ta-yu, Huang-po said, "What a big mouth that old man has. The next time I see him, I'll give him a taste of my staff." Rinzai yelled, "Wait! I'll give it to you right now." And he slapped the old master's face.

The startled Huang-po said, "This crazy monk is plucking the tiger's whiskers."

At that, Rinzai gave his first "Katz!", a shout that would become as famous as Rinzai himself.

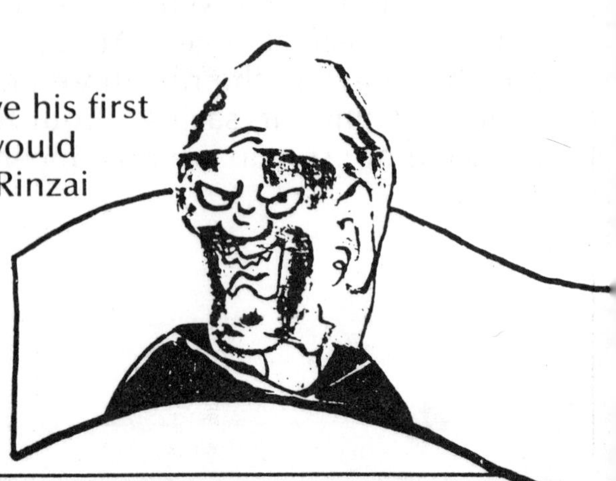

From here on, Rinzai and Huang-po had many sparkling encounters until Rinzai set out on his own, equipped with the transmission and a repertory of punches and shouts, his favorite teaching devices.

He was a true descendant of Ma-tsu, firmly believing that all one needs for enlightenment is the courage to leap into it.

His harsh style got popular partly because it reflected the state China was in at the time. It was 845 and the mounting antagonism towards Buddhism finally burst. Buddhism was accused of destroying the family (Buddhist monks and nuns were celibate) and with it the ancestral line so preciously guarded in this patriarchal society. Buddhism reduced the number of people paying taxes and the number of men able to serve in the army. Furthermore, Chinese nationalism was on an upward swing and Buddhism was resented as an Indian import. The Chinese invested the same vigor in exterminating Buddhism that they had put into establishing it a few centuries earlier.

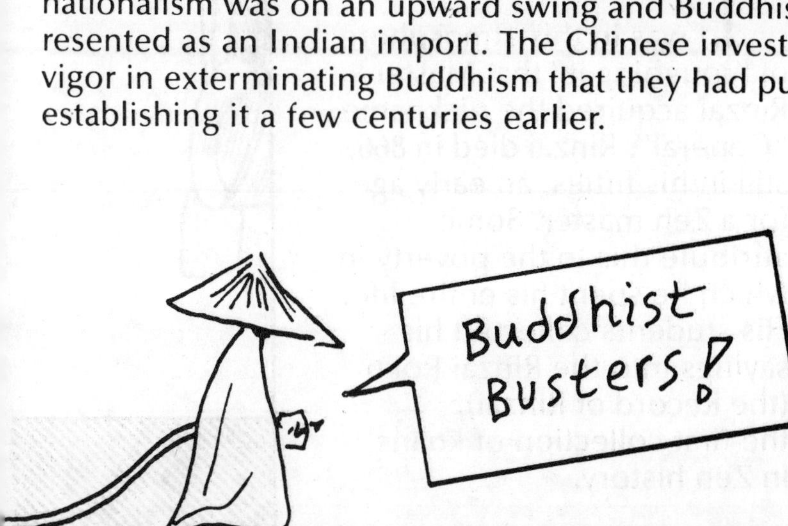

Of all the Buddhist sects in China at that time, only Zen, able to exist without monasteries or religious paraphernalia, survived the persecution.

It was in this atmosphere of "roughing it" that Master Rinzai acquired the nickname, "General". Rinzai died in 866, still in his fifties, an early age for a Zen master. Some attribute this to the poverty in which he spent his entire life. His students collected his sayings into the Rinzai Roku (the Record of Rinzai), the first collection of koans in Zen history.

SOTO

So far we have focused on the descendants of Ma-tsu. But the line of Shih-tou produced some extraordinary masters as well. Among them, Masters Tung-shan (Japanese, Tozan), 807–869, Yun-men (Unmon), 862–949, and Fa-yen (Hogen), 885–958, founded their own schools. Yun-men's descendants compiled the Blue Cliff Record, the largest collection of koans. But today, only Master Tung-shan's line is still alive as the Soto Zen sect.

Tung-shan was a contemporary of Rinzai's ut educated in the Shih-tou style, his teaching echniques were very different. He emphasized azen practice and he was fond of metaphoric inguage to talk his students out of their ntanglements. He is credited with a famous en poem, describing the enlightened realm of penness and spontaneity. Here's one stanza:

His successor, Ts'ao-shun (Jap. Sozan), picked up his style with ease, as we can see from their parting exchange.

"Where are you going?"

"I go where it's changeless."

"How can you go where it's changeless?"

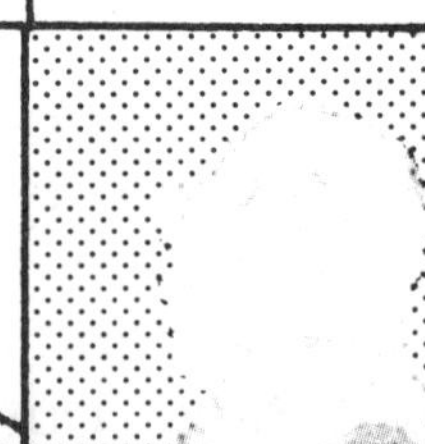

My going is no change

This gentle style and insistence on meditation gave the Soto sect the name "silent illumination path," while the Rinzai sect became known as the "introspecting the koan path."

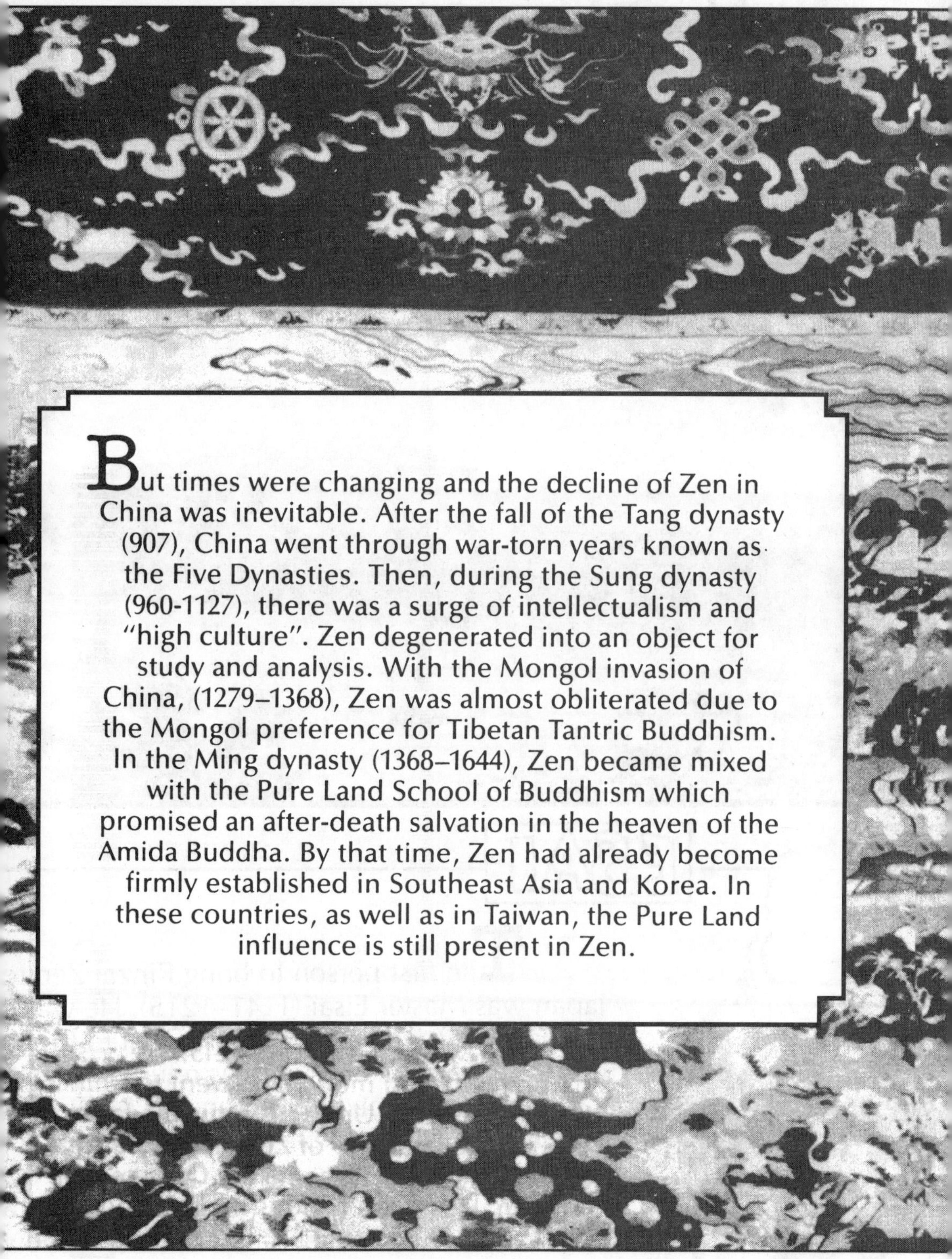

But times were changing and the decline of Zen in China was inevitable. After the fall of the Tang dynasty (907), China went through war-torn years known as the Five Dynasties. Then, during the Sung dynasty (960-1127), there was a surge of intellectualism and "high culture". Zen degenerated into an object for study and analysis. With the Mongol invasion of China, (1279–1368), Zen was almost obliterated due to the Mongol preference for Tibetan Tantric Buddhism. In the Ming dynasty (1368–1644), Zen became mixed with the Pure Land School of Buddhism which promised an after-death salvation in the heaven of the Amida Buddha. By that time, Zen had already become firmly established in Southeast Asia and Korea. In these countries, as well as in Taiwan, the Pure Land influence is still present in Zen.

However, Japanese Zen is closer to the original Zen, because it was transplanted during the Sung dynasty, and then developed in a fairly isolated environment. Here is how it happened:

ESAI

The first person to bring Rinzai Zen to Japan was Master Eisai (1141–1215). He was a Mahayana Buddhist monk who went to China in 1191 to study Zen. Upon his return to Japan, he taught a mixture of Zen and Mahayana Buddhism that would become the Oryo sect of Rinzai Zen. He is also famous for bringing tea to Japan and campaigning to introduce it as a substitute for rice wine (sake). We don't know if he made much profit, but he sure made himself a name. Here is his sales pitch, ancestor of all Hondas, Sonys and Mitsubishis.

"In the great country of China they drink tea, as a result of which there is no heart trouble and people live long lives. Our country is full of sickly-looking skinny persons, and this is simply because we do not drink tea. Whenever one is in poor spirits, one should drink tea. This will put the heart in order and dispel all illness."

The truth is the Rinzai Zen survived in Japan solely because of the fondness which the powerful Samurai had for it. Rinzai's style, hard, illogical, spontaneous and not requiring book learning greatly appealed to them. It fitted their own experience of life: now, or it might be never.

Dogen

But the transplanting of Zen would not have been so successful if not for the appearance of Dogen Kigen (1200–1253), Japan's first great native Zen master, still considered today to be the "most powerful and original thinker Japan has so far produced." The illegitimate son of aristocratic parents, he was well educated in poetry and calligraphy. But his religious journey began right away. His father died when he was two and his mother when he was seven. On her death bed, she made him promise to become a monk. It is said that at her funeral, Dogen wondered at the impermanence of life.

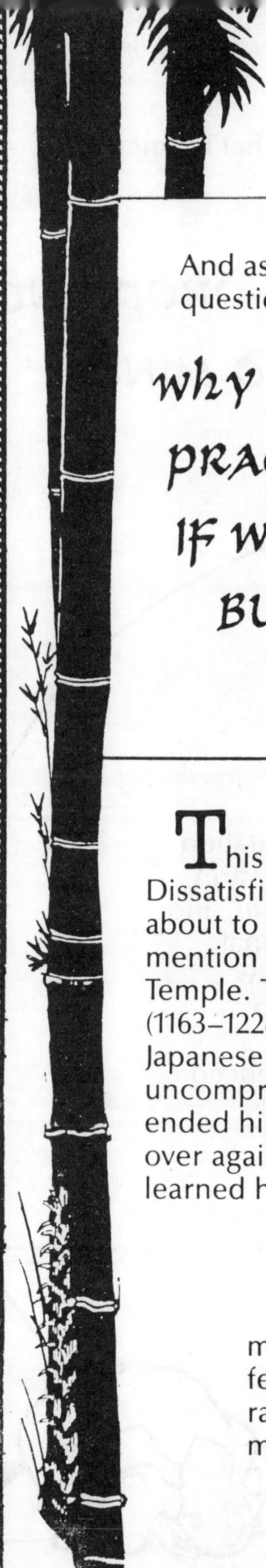

And as a young monk, he was obsessed with the question,

why do we have to practice Buddhism if we already have Buddha nature?

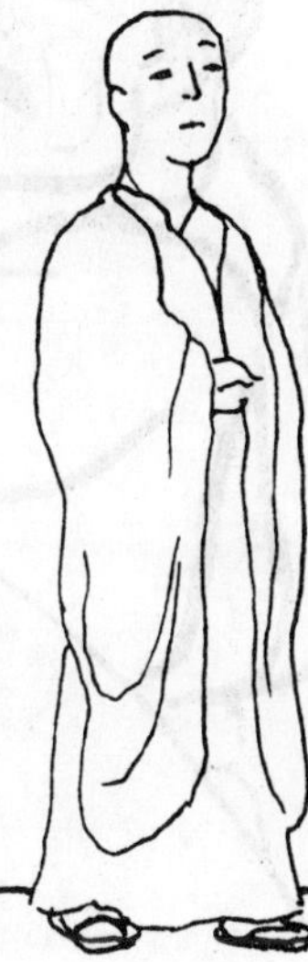

This question brought him eventually to China. Dissatisfied with the discipline he found there, he was about to return home when someone happened to mention to him a new master at the T'ieng T'ung Temple. The meeting of Dogen and this Master Ju-ching (1163–1228) was a fortunate event for the future of Japanese Zen. Ju-ching was a Soto master and an uncompromising advocate of sitting meditation. He ended his daily zazen at eleven at night and started all over again at two-thirty the next morning. Here Dogen learned his Zen and attained his enlightenment.

The story goes that as he was meditating one early morning, the fellow next to him began to doze—a rather common occurrence in modern Zen as well.

Master Ju-ching was passing by at that moment and yelled at the sleeping monk,

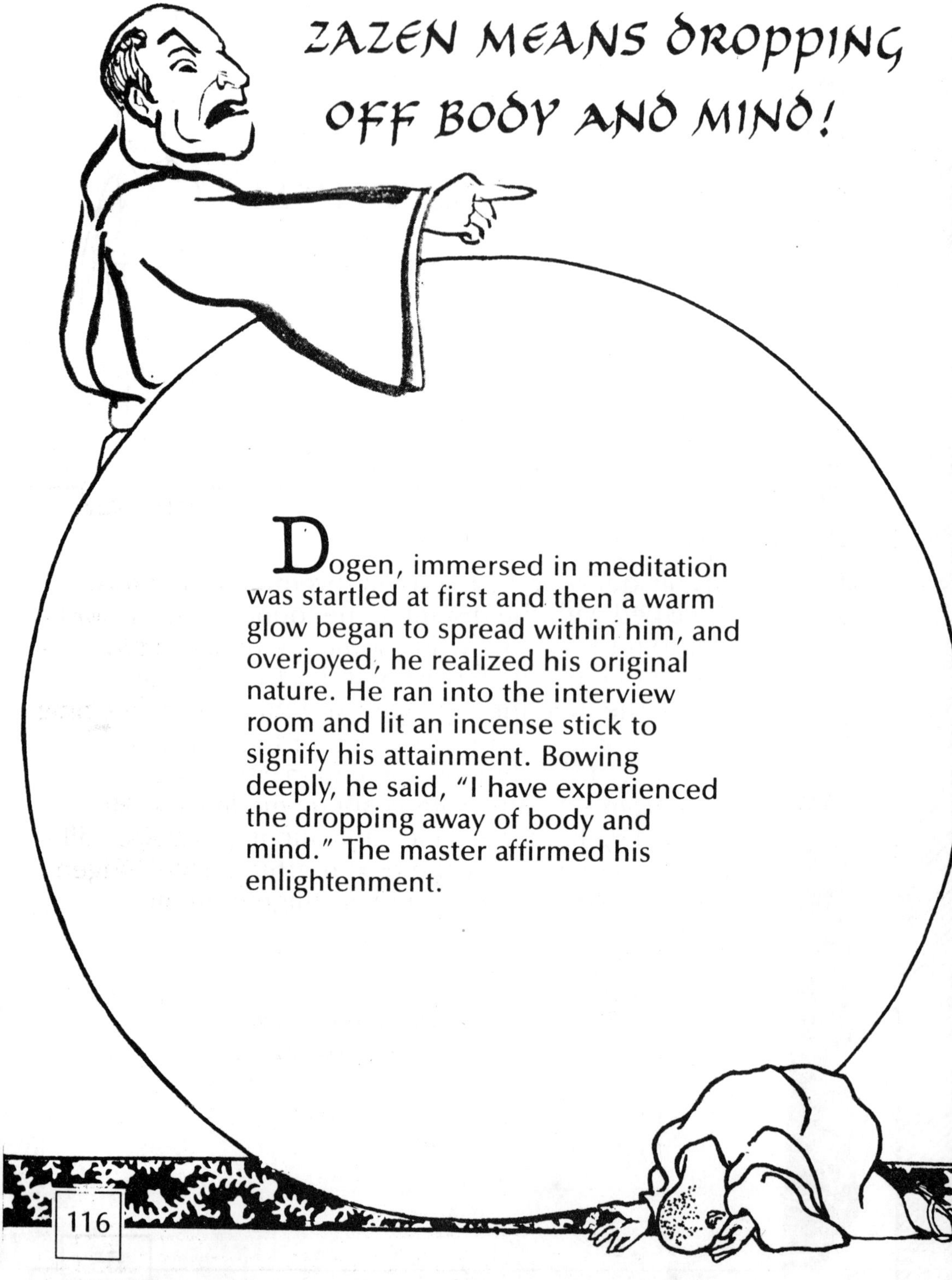

Dogen, immersed in meditation was startled at first and then a warm glow began to spread within him, and overjoyed, he realized his original nature. He ran into the interview room and lit an incense stick to signify his attainment. Bowing deeply, he said, "I have experienced the dropping away of body and mind." The master affirmed his enlightenment.

Dogen stayed with Ju-ching two more years and then journeyed back to Japan, bringing with him Soto Zen. He became a vigorous spokesman for sitting meditation, trying unceasingly to convince his fellow Buddhists that they had better do some zazen or they could forget about enlightenment.

For this purpose, he wrote A Universal Recommendation for Zazen. He says:

You should pay attention to the fact that even the Buddha Sakyamuni had to practice zazen for six years.

It is also said that Bodhidharma had to do zazen at Shao-lin temple for nine years in order to transmit the Buddha-mind. Since these ancient sages were so diligent, how can present-day trainees do without the practice of zazen? You should stop pursuing words and letters and learn to withdraw and reflect on yourself. When you do so, your body and mind will naturally fall away, and your original Buddha nature will appear.

Dogen's followers built him a temple in the mountains called Eihei-ji (Eternal Peace) which is still the center of Japanese Soto Zen today, There he wrote his voluminous Shobogenzo (Treasure of Knowledge Regarding the True Dharma), probably the most complete work ever written about Zen.

Dogen died in 1253. Today the Soto sect has about three times as many followers in Japan as the Rinzai sect.

Hakuin

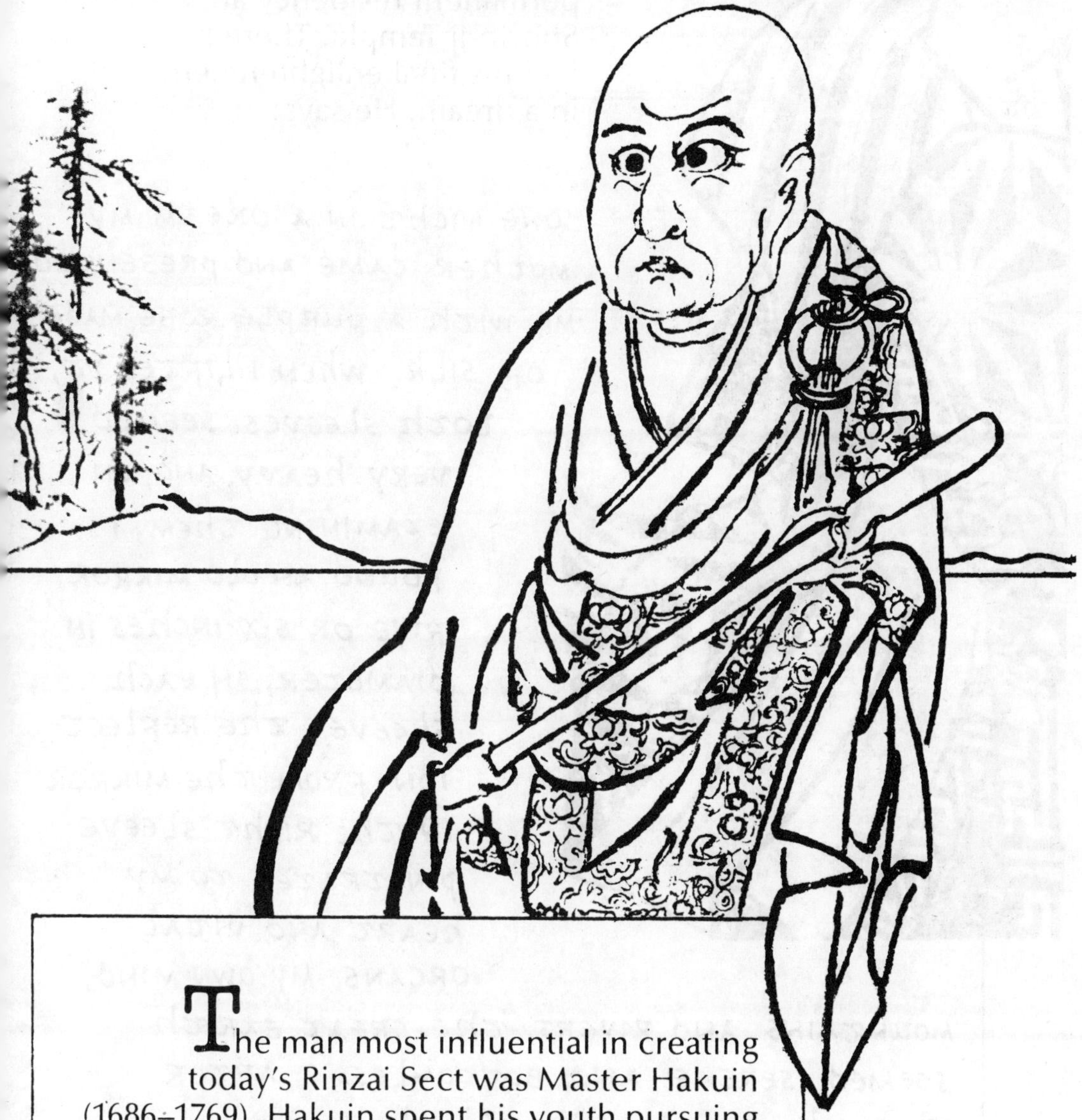

The man most influential in creating today's Rinzai Sect was Master Hakuin (1686–1769). Hakuin spent his youth pursuing enlightenment. He apparently didn't have an easy time of it. He was beaten and laughed at by various masters even after his first satori, which he himself felt was the clearest anyone had had for centuries. But he pushed himself even harder. As a result, he had many deeply enlightening experiences, as well as a nervous breakdown and physical collapse. He sought the help of a Taoist monk and was able to heal himself completely.

He made his permanent residency at Shorin-ji Temple. There he had his final enlightenment in a dream. He says:

One night in a dream my mother came and presented me with a purple robe made of silk. When I lifted it, both sleeves seemed very heavy, and, on examining them, I found an old mirror, five or six inches in diameter, in each sleeve. The reflect-ion from the mirror in the right sleeve penetrated to my heart and vital organs. My own mind, mountains and rivers, the great earth seemed serene and bottomless... After this, when I looked at all things, it was as though I were seeing my own face. For the first time, I understood the saying, "The enlightened spirit sees the Buddha-nature within his eye."

One of Hakuin's main contributions was the idea that one should meditate on the koan even while engaged in daily activity:

WHAT IS THE TRUE MEDITATION?
IT IS TO MAKE EVERYTHING: COUGHING,
SWALLOWING, WAVING THE ARMS,
MOTION, STILLNESS, WORDS, ACTION,
THE EVIL AND THE GOOD,
PROSPERITY AND SHAME,
GAIN AND LOSS, RIGHT AND WRONG,
INTO ONE SINGLE KOAN.

With this, he introduced Zen into the urban life that was developing in Japan at that time.

In his advanced age, he was full of physical vigor. He lectured frequently to several hundred monks, wrote poetry and was famous for his paintings. Towards the end of his life he created the well-known koan for beginners:

WHAT IS THE SOUND OF ONE HAND CLAPPING?

Before leaving the Orient, here's a new koan:

THE WEST

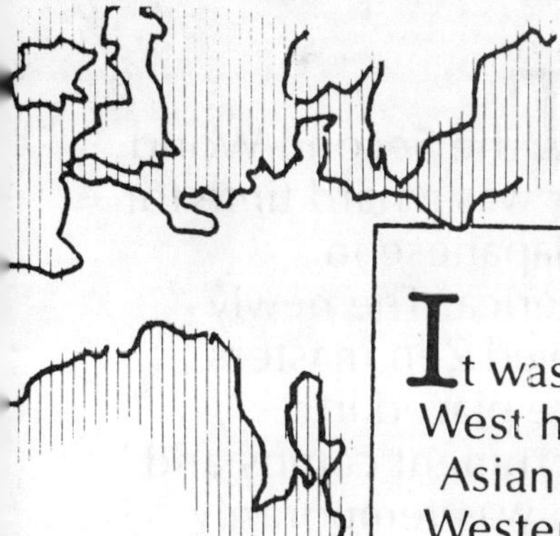

It was not until the late 19th century that the West heard about Zen. At this time, interest in Asian religion in general was growing; some Western philosophers and artists were openly praising Eastern wisdom, and many Eastern texts were translated for the first time into Western languages. The Theosophic Society, founded in 1875, has been an important instrument for spreading the Eastern teaching in the West. In 1893, the first World Parliament of Religion was held in the United States. Among the many delegates from Asian countries was Soyen Shaku from Japan, the first Zen master ever to visit the West. His student, D.T. Suzuki, became the foremost scholarly interpreter of Zen for Westerners. Nyogen Senzaki, another student of Soyen Shaku, settled in Los Angeles. Artist and Zen master, Sokei-an, founded the First Zen Institute of America in New York City originally called The Buddhist Society of America. Ruth Fuller Sasaki, his wife also played an important role in bringing Rinzai Zen to the West. After his death, in 1945, she became a Rinzai Zen priestess at Daitoku-ji temple in Kyoto and established the First Zen Institute of America in Japan.

The Second World War was a hard time for all Japanese in America. The newly arrived Zen masters were placed in internment camps and Zen was temporarily suspended. On being released from the camp, Master Sokei-an observed that "it is by fighting that people come to know each other."

By the fifties, Zen was on an upward swing again. It was the time of the beat generation and many artists turned to Zen for new inspiration. Iconoclasts like Ginsberg, Jack Kerouac, and especially Alan Watts helped make Zen accessible to a wide audience.

By the sixties, there was enough interest and enough teachers to get down to serious practice. Zen centers and monasteries were established both in America and Europe. The Vietnam War caused an influx of Vietnamese Zen teachers on a mission of peace and mindfulness.

In the seventies, Korean Zen teachers brought their own style of Zen, gentle and sparkling. And finally, some Western students earned the privilege of the transmission and continued to spread the Dharma.

Today, Zen centers are nothing unusual in the West. But it is still too early to say the exact form that Zen will take in the wild West.

ZEN and ART

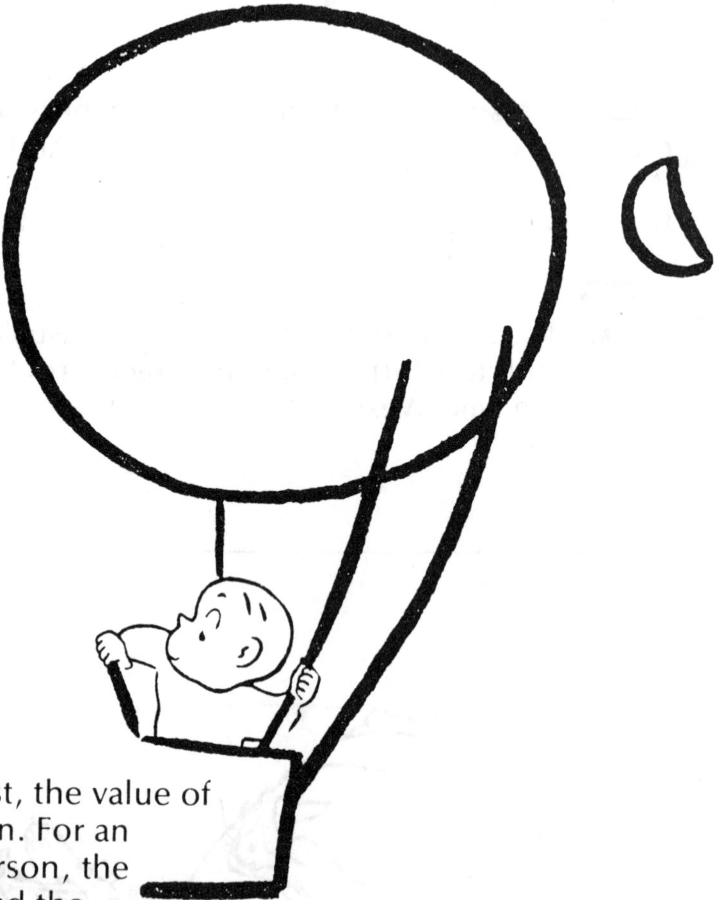

For an artist, the value of life is expression. For an enlightened person, the source of life and the expression of life are identical. The enlightened Zen artist has become one with that source and all of his or her art emerges into the world with the same spontaneity and uniqueness which shapes everything in nature.

For the student of Zen art, the learning process is the same as the process of becoming enlightened. The task is to dissolve the ego, to get out of one's own way.

Here is a quote from Zen in the Art of Archery in which the master is instructing the student archer:

"You can learn from an ordinary bamboo leaf what ought to happen. It bends lower and lower under the weight of snow. Suddenly the snow slips to the ground without the leaf having stirred. Stay like that at the point of highest tension until the shot falls from you. So, indeed it is, when the tension is fulfilled, the shot must fall, it must fall from the archer like snow from a bamboo leaf, before he even thinks it."

It is traditional for a Zen master to express the teaching in poetry and calligraphy. Some, of course, were particularly gifted. Here is a sample from Master Hakuin:

"HEY, BONZE!
WONDER OF WONDERS
YOU'RE DOING ZAZEN TODAY."
"SURE!"

Among the arts which grew out of Zen practice or were greatly influenced by Zen are :

the martial arts

haiku poetry

painting

tea ceremony

Noh drama

flower arranging

pottery

All Zen arts have certain qualities in common. The Japanese use the word "wabi" to describe the loneliness, simplicity and poverty of Zen art. They love objects which look worn or vulnerable, or somehow incomplete, marked by life. The incompleteness and the directness of Zen art involve the audience; our own associations and creativity are called to fill in the gaps.

Here is another example of the very personal content of a Zen poem:

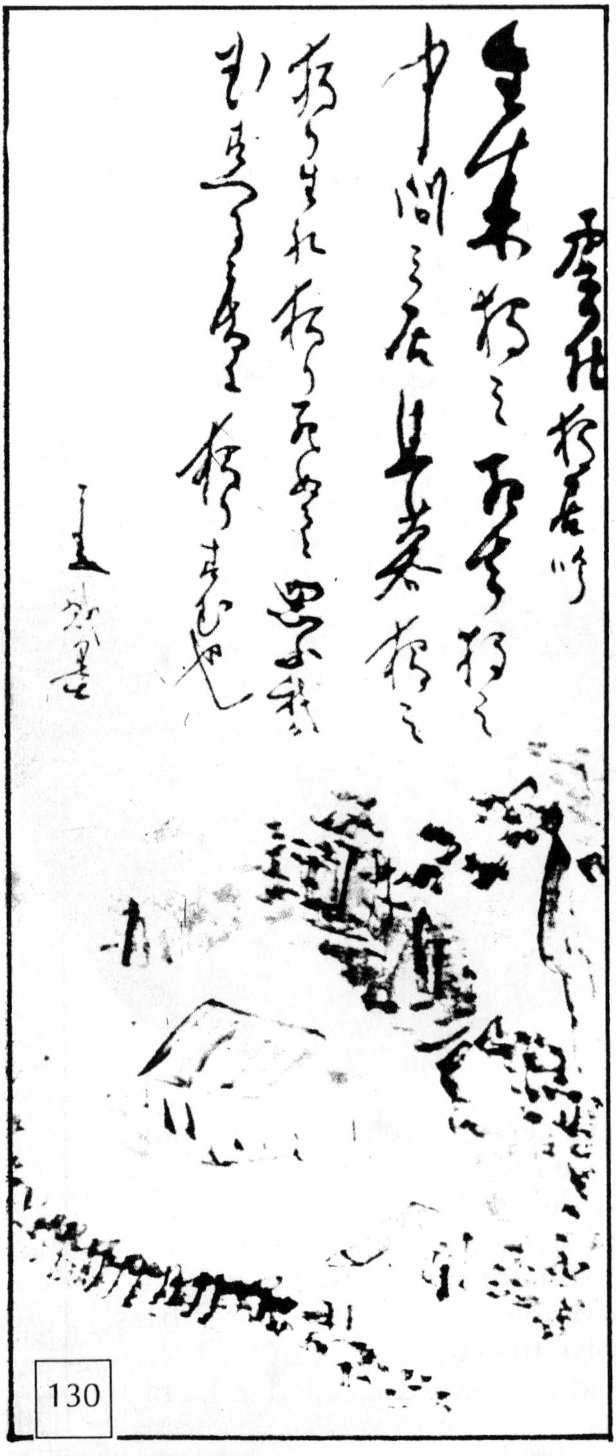

I come alone,
I die alone;
In between times
I am alone day
and night.

-Master Sengai

There are several versions of how the poet Basho wrote his most famous haiku. This one is told by present-day Korean Zen Master Seung Sahn:

"There was once a great Japanese poet named Basho. He was a very bright young man, and as a serious Buddhist he had studied many sutras. He thought that he understood Buddhism. One day he paid a visit to Zen Master Takuan. They talked for a long time. The Master would say something and Basho would respond at length, quoting from the most profound and difficult sutras.

Finally, the Master said,

"You are a great Buddhist, a great man. You understand everything. But in all the time we have been talking, you have only used the words of the Buddha or of eminent teachers. I do not want to hear other people's words. I want to hear your own words, the words of your true self. Quickly now—give me one sentence of your own."

Basho was speechless. His mind raced.

"MY OWN WORDS - WHAT CAN THEY BE?"

"WHAT CAN I SAY?"

One minute passed, then two, then ten. Then the Master said,

I THOUGHT YOU UNDERSTOOD BUDDHISM. WHY CAN'T YOU ANSWER ME?

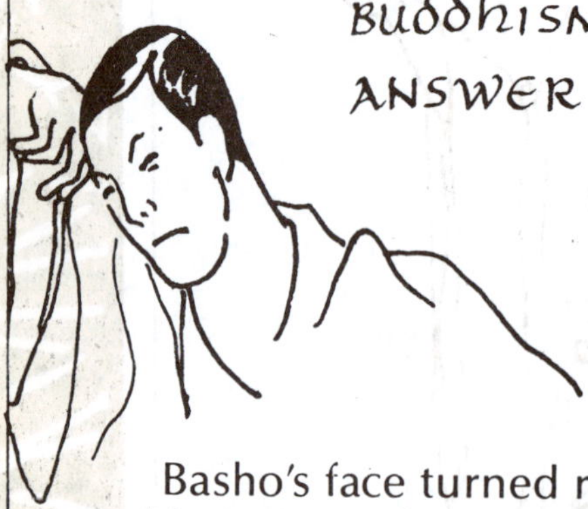

Basho's face turned red. His mind stopped short. It could not move left or right, forward or back. It was up against an impenetrable wall. Then, only vast emptiness.

Suddenly, there was a sound in the monastery garden. Basho turned to the Master and said,

still pond
a frog jumps in
kerplunk!

The Master laughed out loud and said,

"well now! these are
the words of your true self!"

Basho laughed too. He had attained enlightenment.

the
end."

And here, another frog stars in a haiku, this one by Kikaku (1660–1707):

A LITTLE FROG
RIDING ON A BANANA LEAF,
TREMBLING.

Dr. R.H. Blyth, an authority on haiku, gives this explanation for their power:

EACH THING IS PREACHING THE LAW (DHARMA) INCESSANTLY, BUT THIS LAW IS NOT SOMETHING DIFFERENT FROM THE THING ITSELF. HAIKU IS THE REVEALING OF THIS PREACHING BY PRESENTING US WITH THE THING DEVOID OF ALL OUR MENTAL TWISTING AND EMOTIONAL DISCOLORATION, OR RATHER, IT SHOWS THE THING AS IT EXISTS AT ONE AND THE SAME TIME OUTSIDE AND INSIDE THE MIND, PERFECTLY SUBJECTIVE, OURSELVES UNDIVIDED FROM THE OBJECT, THE OBJECT IN ITS ORIGINAL UNITY WITH OURSELVES...

IT IS A WAY OF RETURNING TO
NATURE, TO OUR MOON NATURE,
OUR CHERRY-BLOSSOM NATURE,
OUR FALLING LEAF NATURE,
IN SHORT, TO OUR BUDDHA NATURE.

IT IS A WAY IN WHICH THE
COLD WINTER RAIN,
THE SWALLOWS OF EVENING,
EVEN THE VERY DAY IN ITS
HOTNESS AND THE LENGTH
OF THE NIGHT BECOME
TRULY ALIVE, SHARE IN OUR
HUMANITY, SPEAK THEIR OWN
SILENT AND EXPRESSIVE LANGUAGE.

It was Hojo Tokiyori (1227–1263), Kamakura era warlord in Japan who first realized the value that Zen would have for the Samurai's training. Thereafter, the Samurai Shoguns became the main sponsors of Zen. It was said that in order to attain mastery in swordsmanship, it was necessary for the Samurai to transcend death while still alive. He had to learn to face death unflinchingly. Zen masters soon realized that they could teach Zen to their warrior disciples through the medium of swordsmanship. Here is how Master Takuan instructed the great Samurai, Yagyu Tajima:

No doubt you see the sword about to strike you, but do not let your mind stop there. Have no intention to counter-attack him in response to his threatening move, cherish no calculating thoughts whatever. You simply perceive the opponent's move.

you do not allow your
mind to stop with it,
you move on just as you
are toward the opponent and make
use of his attack by turning it on
himself. then his sword meant to
kill you will become your own and
the weapon will fall on the
opponent himself.

and–

try not to localize the mind anywhere,
but let it fill up the whole body,
let it flow throughout the
totality of your being. when this
happens you use the hands where
they are needed, you use the legs or
the eyes where they are needed,
and no time or energy will go
to waste.

Today these principles form the foundation of Aikido and all other martial arts.

The style of painting associated with Zen in Japan is Sumiye brush painting. The aesthetic requirements of Sumiye are well defined. Foremost is the ability to transmit one's spiritual energy into the painting. This is a matter of immediacy and spontaneity of experience. Once a brushstroke is made, it cannot be corrected. Paintings are sketchy, simple and almost bare. Contrast is emphasized in the black ink on the white background, and the poignant liveliness of objects against the bare vast emptiness of the space behind them. There are no premeditated rules of symmetry or perspective, and dynamism is emphasized rather than shape.

The Chinese painter Chin Nung once said:

YOU PAINT THE BRANCH WELL
AND YOU HEAR THE WIND.

And the Zen Master Ikkyu wrote:

AND WHAT IS IT, THE HEART?
IT IS THE SOUND OF THE PINE BREEZE
IN THE INK PAINTING.

One of the most traditional forms of Zen art is the death poem or "gata"–a stanza of four lines which Zen masters would write to summarize their teaching for their students shortly before assuming the crosslegged zazen position and passing on. Here is how some of them handled this auspicious moment:

what shall be my legacy?
the blossoms of spring,
the cuckoo in the hills,
the leaves of autumn."

—master ryokan

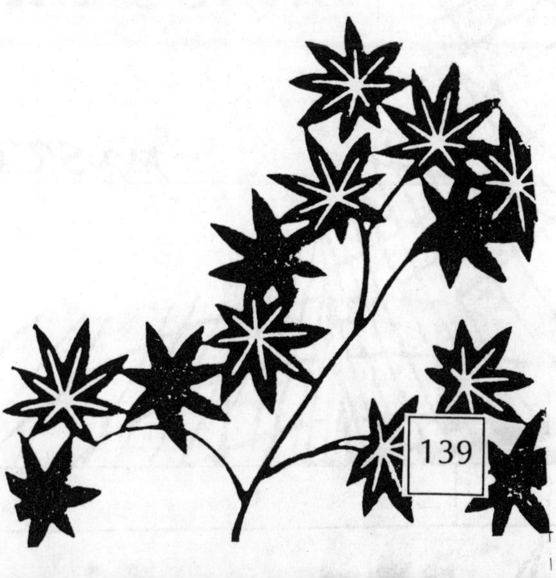

ONE MASTER, WHEN "PRESSED"
FOR HIS GATA, FINALLY RESPONDED WITH:

LIFE IS THUS
DEATH IS THUS
GATA OR NOT GATA,
WHAT'S THE FUSS?

–MASTER?

Another Master showed a true sense of Zen practicality. He wrote sixty postal cards on the last day of his life, and asked his attendant to mail them. Then he sat down on his cushion and died. The cards read:

ZEN IN DAILY LIFE

Zen teaches singlemindedness, wholeheartedness, intimacy, direct perception, non-aggression and spontaneity—a total transformation of our whole being and behavior, affecting all aspects of our life.

Because Zen Buddhists believe that everything is constantly changing, they practice opening themselves to the natural flow of life, instead of trying to hold onto the past or manipulate the future.

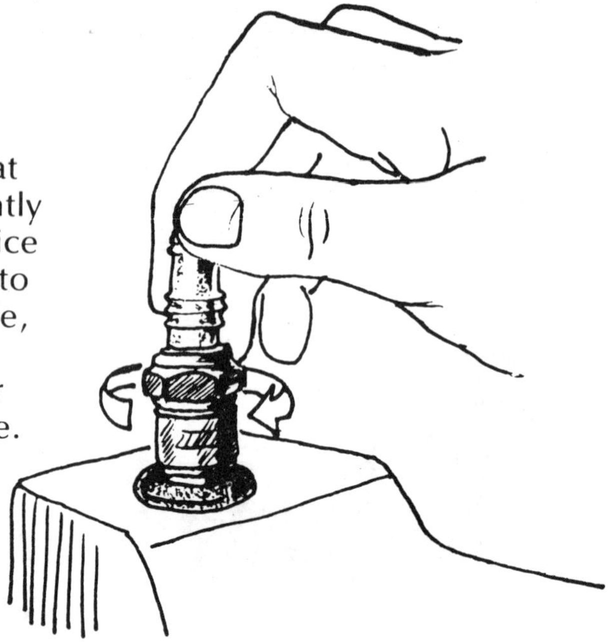

This is called non-clinging or non-grasping. It is also called "following an arrow around a tree."

Buddhist monks used to beg every day for their meals in order to cultivate an attitude of humility and acceptance. It is said that Buddha died from eating poisonous meat which he'd received begging.

The third Patriarch of Zen, Seng-ts'an, said: THE GREAT WAY IS VERY SIMPLE. JUST AVOID PICKING AND CHOOSING.

In other words, there is a greater (realer) dimension of reality beyond our own ideas of good and bad. Because all comparisons are imposed on the world by our conceptual mind, we can never say that one form is actually superior to another. All forms are part of a single fabric of life. The Zen student is careful not to make judgments which limit experience, which split up this wholeness.

The following story of Master Hakuin is an illustration of non-clinging:

The Zen Master Hakuin was praised by his neighbors as one living a pure life. A beautiful girl whose parents owned a food store lived near him. Suddenly without warning, her parents discovered she was pregnant. This made them very angry. The girl would not confess who the father was, but, after much harrassment, at last named Hakuin.

The enraged parents went to the master. "Is that so?", was all he would say.

After the child was born, it was brought to Hakuin. By this time, he had lost his reputation, which did not trouble him, but he took very good care of the child. He obtained milk from his neighbors, and everything else the little one needed.

A year later, the girl-mother could stand it no longer. She told her parents the truth—that the real father of the child was a young man who worked in the fish market.

The parents of the girl at once went to the master to ask his forgiveness, to apologize at length, and to get the child back again. Hakuin was willing. In yielding the child, all he said was, "Is that so?"

Just as the mind runs through the whole universe, it runs through the whole body. A conflicted mind is reflected in a poorly coordinated body. The more the mind is balanced in zazen, the more balanced the body becomes, and this causes the accumulation of energy, called in Zen joriki. So zazen directly affects all of our activities, the way we walk, the way we gesture, the way we speak. There is a story that once when a group of monks had gathered to hear Master Fa-yen give a discourse: instead of speaking he pointed at the bamboo curtains. Two monks at the same time went to roll them up. The master said, "One has gained, one has lost." The directness and power of the action reveals to an enlightened eye the depth of the student's understanding.

Zen practice also affects the way we interact with other people. Master Rinzai said that people are always in one of these three relationships to each other:

1 Host and Guest

The host is in touch with reality and the guest is confused.

2 Guest and Guest

Neither one knows what's going on.

3 Host and Host

Both are enlightened. This is said to be like "two thieves meeting in the night. They know each other immediately."

Master Rinzai said, *Followers of the Way, he who is now listening to the Dharma, he is not the four elements; he is the one who can use the four elements. If you can see it thus, then you are free in your coming and going.*

An accomplished Zen student is always master of the situation, completely free to respond in any way. At the same time, he or she is totally involved in whatever is happening.

Modern Roshi Philip Kapleau writes that there are two stages of this involvement, mindfulness and mindlessness.

These are simply two different degrees of absorption.

Mindfulness is a state wherein one is totally aware in any situation and so always able to respond appropriately. Yet one is aware of being aware.

Mindlessness, on the other hand, or "no-mindness" as it has been called, is a condition of such complete absorption that there is no vestige of self-awareness.

An early Buddhist Sutra says:

In what is seen, there must just be the seen; in what is heard, there must just be the heard; in what is sensed, there must just be the sensed; in what is thought, there must just be the thought.

It is just this pure, direct reception of life which finally reveals ultimate reality, the one mind of the universe, to the Zen student.

A monk said to the Master, "Please show me the way to enlightenment." The master said, "Do you hear the murmuring sound of the mountain stream?" The monk said, "Yes, I do." "Enter there", said the Master.

One of the most distinctive aspects of Zen teaching is its insistence on self-reliance. Zen teaches that we are each the Buddha. Since that is our real nature, there is nothing we have to do to become the Buddha (although there's often a lot of stuff for us to stop doing). The Zen student is expected to develop self-respect (for this real self) even beyond respect for the formalities of Zen. Here are three quotes from Master Rinzai on this theme:.

In my talks there is absolutely nothing real. If you see it thus, you can spend ten thousand pieces of yellow gold a day – enjoy yourself!

O brethren of the way, you must know that in the reality of Buddhism there is nothing extraordinary for you to perform. You just live as usual without even trying to do anything in particular, attending to your natural wants, putting on clothes, eating meals, and lying down when you feel tired.

Let ignorant people laugh at me, the wise know what I mean to say.

And—

Followers of the Way, do not take the Buddha as the supreme aim. I myself see him as a privy hole and the Bodhisattvas as beings who bind men with chains.

On the same theme, the 4th Patriarch, Tao-hsin said:

There is nothing lacking in you and you yourself are no different from the Buddha. There is no other way of achieving Buddhahood than letting your mind free to be itself.

So the Zen student is not trying to transcend, or to get away from nature. Our actual nature is the thing sought and realized by the enlightened person.

Zen is a completely experiential religion. Rather than being instructed in how things are or should be, the student is given techniques for achieving his or her own understanding and sensation of reality. Zen has been compared to drinking a glass of water. You cannot know the taste without tasting it yourself. This firsthand experience gives the advanced Zen student a firm self-confidence.

There is a story about a 5th century Zen master named Tao-sheng who had this kind of confidence. During his lifetime in China, Buddhist teachers did not think that all forms could be said to have Buddha nature, regardless of their consciousness. Tao-sheng was sure that everything does have Buddha nature and for this, he was expelled from the Buddhist community as a heretic. Later when the complete Nirvana Sutra was translated into Chinese, it was found that Buddha had taught that all forms do have Buddha nature. But at that time, Tao-sheng trusted his intuition so strongly that he was content to lecture on the subject to the rocks in the field. The story goes that the rocks nodded in perfect agreement with the master. Years later, a Master Ungan remarked that the rocks were nodding long before anyone bothered to speak to them.

We're going to end this book with some sound advice from the venerable Master Rinzai on how to achieve what was never lost—complete enlightenment:

"I tell you this: there is no Buddha, no Dharma, no training and no realization. What are you so hotly chasing? Putting a head on top of your head, you blind fools? Your head is right where it should be. What are you lacking? Followers of the Way, the one functioning right here before your eyes, he is not different from the Buddhas and Patriarchs. But you do not believe it, and so turn to the outside to seek. Be not deceived. If you turn to the outside, there is no Dharma; neither is there anything to be obtained from the inside. Rather than attaching yourselves to my words, better calm down and seek nothing further. Do not cling to the past, nor hanker after the future. This is better than a ten years' pilgrimage."

what is the way?
GO!

NOTES

1. Early History

p. 38 - quoted from Seng-ts'an, "Verses on the Faith of the Mind."

p. 46-48 - quotes on Hui-neng from D.T. Suzuki, _Zen Buddhism_ (New York: Doubleday, 1956).

2. Zen Principles

p. 54 - Rinzai quote from _Towards a Philosophy of Zen Buddhism_ by T. Izutsu (Boulder: Great Eastern, 1982).

p. 56 - Huai-hai quote from T. Hoover, _The Zen Experience_ (New York;: New American Library, 1980).

p. 57 - Seppo quote from D.T. Suzuki, op. cit.

p. 58-59 - The twentieth century Zen master is Yasutani Roshi.

ZEN PRINCIPLES CON'T

p. 60 – THE CONTEMPORARY ZEN MASTER IS JOSHU SASAKI ROSHI.

p. 62-63 – THE HEAVEN AND HELL ANECDOTE IS FROM P. REP'S, *ZEN FLESH, ZEN BONES* (NEW YORK: DOUBLEDAY, 1980).

p. 65-66 – HOGEN STORY, IBID.

3. ZEN PRACTICE

p. 76 – THE PORTRAITS OF JOSHU AND THE MONK ARE BASED ON TWO PHOTOS OF GESTALT THERAPIST DANIEL ROSENBLATT, THE ILLUSTRATOR'S UNCLE, AND THEY ARE HIS 60TH BIRTHDAY PRESENT.

p. 77 – MU COMMENTS QUOTED FROM K. YAMADA, *THE GATELESS GATE* (INDIANAPOLIS: CENTER PUBLISHING, 1980).

ZEN PRACTICE CON'T.

p. 82 - MA-TSU'S COMMENT ON PRECEPTS FROM T. HOOVER, OP. CIT.

p. 85 - THE R.H. BLYTH QUOTE, FROM ZEN AND ZEN CLASSICS, VOLUME 2 (TOKYO: HOKUSEIDO PRESS, 1964), WAS SELECTED BY THE ILLUSTRATOR, AND INCLUDED UNBEKNOWNST TO THE AUTHORS.

p. 92 - THE CONTEMPORARY ROSHI IS JOSHU SASAKI ROSHI, AND THE RINZAI QUOTES ARE FROM I. SCHLOEGEL, THE ZEN TEACHINGS OF RINZAI (BOULDER: SHAMBALA PUBLICATIONS, 1976).

4. LATER HISTORY

ALL STORIES ARE FROM T. HOOVER, OP. CIT.

p. 123 - CONTEMPORARY HISTORY NOTES FROM R. FIELDS, AND FROM MARY FARKAS.

5. ZEN AND ART

p.127 - quote from E. Herrigel, ZEN AND THE ART OF ARCHERY (New York: Random House, 1971).

p.128 - Hakuin poem from I. Miura and R.F. Sasaki ZEN DUST. (New York: Harcourt, Brace, Jovanovich).

p.129 - the arranged flower sketch included courtesy of Ingrid Homberg, "Blumen Flowers."

p.130 - poem by Sengai from T. Izutsu, op. cit. The image is a drawing, with that poem calligraphed in Japanese, by Sengai and reproduced from D.T. Suzuki SENGAI THE ZEN MASTER (Shinkokai: Kokusai Bunka, 1961).

p.131-3 - Basho story from Seung Sahn Soen Sa-Nim, Dropping Ashes on the Buddha (New York: Grove Press, 1976).

ZEN AND ART CON'T.

p. 134 – POEM BY KIKAKU QUOTED FROM D.T. SUZUKI, ZEN AND JAPANESE CULTURE (PRINCETON UNIVERSITY PRESS, 1959).

p. 135 – BLYTH QUOTE FROM R.H. BLYTH, HAIKU (SOUTH SAN FRANCISCO: HEIAN INTERNATIONAL).

p. 136-7 – QUOTES FROM D.T. SUZUKI, ZEN AND JAPANESE CULTURE, OP. CIT.

p. 140 – GATA FROM P. REP, OP. CIT.

6. ZEN IN DAILY LIFE

p. 146-7 HAKUIN STORY FROM P. REP, OP. CIT.

p. 148 FA-YEN (HOGEN) STORY FROM K. YAMADA, OP. CIT.

ZEN IN DAILY LIFE CON'T.

p. 151 – RINZAI QUOTE FROM
I. SCHLOEGEL, OP. CIT.

p. 152 – SUTRA QUOTE FROM P. KAPLEAU,
THREE PILLARS OF ZEN
(NEW YORK: DOUBLEDAY, 1980).

p. 152 – "MURMURING SOUND" FROM
T. IZUTSU, OP. CIT.

p. 153-4 – RINZAI AND TAO-HSIN QUOTE
FROM T. HOOVER, OP. CIT.

p. 157 – TAO-SHENG STORY FROM D.T.
SUZUKI, ZEN BUDDHISM, OP. CIT.

p. 158 – RINZAI QUOTES FROM I. SCHLOEGEL,
OP. CIT.

GLOSSARY

Bodhi—Enlightenment (Sanskrit)
Bodhisattva—One who vows not to enter Nirvana before liberating all sentient beings (Sans.)
Buddhahood—A complete enlightenment (Sans.)
Dhyana—Meditation (Sans.)
Gasho—Placing the palms of hands together, a sign of respect (Jap.)
Gata—A short four line poem (Jap.)
Hara—The source of vital energy in the navel area focused on in Zen meditation (Jap.)
Hinayana—The lesser vehicle, the path of solitary realizers (Sans.)
Joriki—The power of concentration; Also: Reliance on oneself for liberation, as opposed to Thriki—reliance on other (Jap.)
Jukai—Lay ordination (Jap.)
Karma—Action; Also: Law of the cause and effect (Sans.)
Kensho—Insight into one's own nature; also called Satori (Jap.)
Koan—"Public Record," a documented instance of interaction between Master and student. (Jap.)
Kinhin—Walking meditation (Jap.)
Kyosaku—A stick used to prevent dozing in meditation hall, as well as for a general refreshment (Jap.)
Makyo—A hallucination (Jap.)
Nirvana—Extinction of craving, frustration and ignorance (Sans.)
Samsara—Wordly existence, that is craving, frustration and ignorance (Sans.)
Rakasu—A rectangular piece of cloth worn on one's chest (Jap.)
Roshi—A teacher (Jap.)
Sesshin—Intensive meditation retreat (Jap.)
Skandhas—The aggregates a person is made of: form, feeling, perception, conception, consciousness (Sans.)
Shikan-Taza—A form of Zen meditation without an object of concentration (Jap.)
Sutra—Buddhist scripture (Sans.)
Three Treasures—Are Buddha, Dharma and Sangha. Buddha is the ultimate truth; Dharma is the teaching about it; and the Sangha is the community of people practicing the teachings.
Tathagata—One who has come to truth (Sans.)
Zazen—Zen meditation (Jap.)
Zendo—Meditation hall (Jap.)

BIBLIOGRAPHY

Blyth, R.H. *Zen and Zen Classics, Volumes I–V*. San Francisco: Heian International, 1982.

Burtt, Edwin A., ed. *Teachings of the Compassionate Buddha*. New York: New American Library, 1955.

Herrigel, Eugen. *Zen in the Art of Archery*. New York: Random House, 1971.

Hoover, Thomas. *Zen Experience*. New York: New American Library, 1980.

Izutsu, T. *Toward a Philosophy of Zen Buddhism*. Boulder: Great Eastern, 1982.

Kapleau, Philip. *Three Pillars of Zen: Teaching, Practice, Enlightenment*. New York: Doubleday, 1980.

Maezumi, Hakuyu T., and Glassman, Bernard T. *Hazy Moon of Enlightenment: On Zen Practice III*. Indianapolis: Center Publishing, 1978.

Merton, Thomas. *Zen and the Birds of Appetite*. New York: New Directions, 1968.

Merton, Thomas. *Mystics and Zen Masters*. New York: Delta, 1961.

Miura, Isshu and Sasaki, Ruth F. *Zen Koan*. New York: Harcourt, Brace, Jovanovich, 1966.

Price, A.F., and Mou-lam. *Diamond Sutra and the Sutra of Hui Neng*. Boulder: Shambhala Publications, 1969.

Ross, Nancy Wilson. *Buddhism: A Way of Life and Thought*. New York: Random House, 1980.

Rep, Paul, ed. *Zen Flesh, Zen Bones: A Collection of Zen and Pre-Zen Writings*. New York: Doubleday, 1980.

Sahn, Seung. *Dropping Ashes on the Buddha: The Teaching of Zen Master Seung Sahn*. Trans. Stephen Mitchell. New York: Grove Press, 1976.

Schloegl, Irmgard. *Zen Teaching of Rinzai*. Boulder: Shambhala Publications, 1976.

Suzuki, D.T. *Zen Buddhism: Selected Writings of D.T. Suzuki*. New York: Doubleday, 1956.

Suzuki, D.T. *Zen and Japanese Culture*. Princeton: Princeton University Press, 1959.

Suzuki, Shunryu. *Zen Mind, Beginner's Mind*. Weatherhill, 1970.

Watts, Alan W. *The Way of Zen*. New York: Vintage Books, 1957.

Yamada, Koun. *Gateless Gate*. Indianapolis: Center Publishing, 1980.

JUDITH BLACKSTONE AND ZORAN JOSIPOVIC

have been students of Zen and other Eastern forms of meditation for many years. They have lived and practiced at the Zen Mountain Monastery in Mt. Tremper, NY and at Chogye International Zen Center in New York City. They are directors of Realization Center in Woodstock, NY where they offer meditation, psychotherapy and bodywork. They can be reached at PO Box 1209, Woodstock, NY 12498.

NAOMI ROSENBLATT

was born in 1957, and began drawing a couple of years later. A graduate of The Cooper Union and New York University, Naomi has shown paintings and prints in the New York area where she generally lives, and works as a muralist. This is her first illustrated work (more in the series to come). Naomi is not a Zen disciple, but has encountered Zen teachings through studying Asian art.

Authors would like to express their appreciation to:

John Daido Loori
Zen Mountain Monastery,
Mount Tremper, NY

and

Mary Farkas
First Zen Institute of America
New York, NY

for their assistance.

the illustrator thanks:

the carrolls, for lending me their sengai catalogue and calendar, which were indispensable.

the pageant book and print shop 109 east 9th street.

my art director, janet siefert, for excellent advice.

our editor, glenn thompson, for endless patience, flexibility and vision.

our general manager, ann shields, for tireless work and perspicacity.

